ANNA IN THE TROPICS

BY NILO CRUZ

D0971733

★

★

DRAMATISTS
PLAY SERVICE
INC.

ANNA IN THE TROPICS
Copyright © 2003, Nilo Cruz

All Rights Reserved

SPECIAL NOTE

Roger Berlind, Daryl Roth, Ray Larsen, in association with Robert Bartner presented the New York premiere of *Anna in the Tropics* at the Royale Theatre.

Anna in the Tropics was originally commissioned and produced by New Theatre, Coral Gables, FL, Rafael de Acha, Artistic Director; Eileen Suarez, Managing Director, through a residency grant from Theatre Communications Group and the National Endowment for the Arts.

It was subsequently produced by South Coast Repertory, Costa Mesa, CA, David Emmes, Producing Artistic Director; Paula Tomei, Managing Director, and at the McCarter Theatre Center, Princeton, NJ, Emily Mann, Artistic Director; Jeffrey Woodward, Managing Director. The McCarter Theatre Center production transferred to Broadway.

*My special appreciation and gratitude to Janice Paran
for her wisdom and advice in helping me
restructure the second act of this play.*

THE ALPHABET OF SMOKE

My fascination with the world of cigars started with cigar boxes and cigar labels. These wooden boxes, with their intricate pictures of imaginary landscapes, suggested the possibility of escaping to a magical place through the brevity of a smoke. They have always intrigued me. Cigar brands have a certain allure, since some of them have been named after the greatest ill-fated love stories ever written; as if the smoker is to experience the enraptured heights of romantic passion from a puff of a Romeo y Julieta or a Madame Butterfly.

When I was commissioned to write a play for New Theatre in Coral Gables, Florida, I immediately turned to the world of cigars. The first thing I did was place an old cigar box in front of me to invite the writing into my hands. I stared at the simple box for a long time, paying close attention to all its details. It seemed like all the ingredients I needed for my play were in this container: love, literature, politics and loss of innocence; themes I had explored in the past through my plays. And, as it always happens, I had to close my eyes so I could dream up the world I was going to write about. The first image that came to me was that of a lector (a reader) reading aloud to cigar workers in Tampa. The second image was of a woman in the same cigar factory escaping the monotony of work through the story that was being read. As these images became more clear, I started to find my way back in time to the late 1920s, when the world of art played an important role in the *tabaquerias* (factories) as the *lectores* read to workers from world literature.

My association with cigars has always been related to escape. As a child in Cuba I was given a cigar box for my coloring pencils. The United States embargo and the scarcity of food and material goods forced Cubans to embrace the concept of recycling. Objects were assigned multiple functions and responsibilities. My cigar box, with its landscape label of palm trees and women draped in flowing *tulles*, became more than a pencil box. It became my box of dreams — my Houdini box — in which I was able to escape from everything happening around me.

The early sixties in Cuba was a time of political unrest and uncertainty — it seemed like everyone in my house created their own circus act in order to escape reality. Cigar smoke offered my father escape from his disenchantment with the revolution. The smoke rings out of his mouth (seemed like circus rings to me) were more like smoke signals asking his friends in the States for political asylum. My mother had her own circus act. She used to find escape through prayer, and used cigar smoke as a celestial envelope to send her supplications to the Divine. Her altar consisted of Catholic saints and African deities. She made her own incense by inserting the burning end of the cigar into her mouth and exhaling her breath through it. The result was a surge of smoke that bathed all her sacred statues in a blue cloud. I believed these mystifying smoke rituals to be truly miraculous when my family was finally allowed to flee the country in 1970.

Literary reveries are related to cigar smoke — both permit one to escape the weight of the world and defy the laws of gravity. Cigar workers were able to escape the monotony of manual labor through literary reveries. The art of listening to stories is analogous with dreaming: the listener collects words and draws pictures in his mind; the dreamer collects subconscious impressions and paints vivid images in his dreams. Literary reveries provide the listener with information about his individual essence and create emotional parallels to his own life; dreams present the dreamer with a series of images and symbols that mirror his present life or past existence. Perhaps these imaginary flights don't offer immediate solutions to life's difficulties, but to pause over a few lines of a book and share human emotion can bring a sense of consolation and alleviate reality.

The tradition of having *lectores* in the cigar factories can be traced back to the Taino Indians. For the Native Americans of Cuba the sacred tobacco leaf was tied to the language of the gods. The leaves were smoked or converted into powder that was mixed with pulverized seashells. This fusion of ingredients was known as *cohoba,* and it was smoked or inhaled through the nose. The *cacique* (Indian chief) used to communicate with the Divine through this sacred concoction. A well-known Spanish colonialist, Bartolomé de Las Casas, described the indigenous rite in Chapter CLXVI of his *Apologética historia*: "And I witnessed how they celebrated the *cohoba* and it was extraordinary to see how they took it and what they said ... The one who began was the *cacique* and all the rest remained quiet until he was finished; once he had consumed his *cohoba,* he held his head to one side for some time with his arms over his knees, and then he raised his face toward the sky speaking certain words, which could have been a prayer." In the cigar factories, the lector became a sort of *cacique* who gave voice to the written words, and the cigar rollers became listeners who wrapped the spoken words in cigar leaves as their minds wandered to the heights of literature.

The days at the cigar factories were divided into three parts: in the morning the *lectores* read from newspaper articles, in the afternoon they read from the proletarian press, and the last part of the day was saved for the sweet delicacy of the novel. Besides providing literary escape, the *lectores* were instrumental in facilitating awareness and mobilizing change in the workplace and the larger political arena. Cuba's greatest poet and political leader, José Martí, read in the cigar factories of Tampa in the late 1800s. He believed that people who attended literary events were the ones who promoted ethics in politics and preserved the nation's honor. He was a firm believer that the purpose of literature was to help humanity, and that one could not know a country without knowing its literature.

Cigar laborers were mostly illiterate, but they could recite passages from *Don Quixote*, or a verse by Rubén Darío. These workers were similar to musicians who can't read music but can play it by ear. They demanded precision from the *lectores* and elicited coloratura in their reading. Factory owners did not hire the *lectores*, the workers did. In the same way that an actor or an opera singer auditions for a role, the *lectores* had to audition before a group of cigar workers. A strong voice was imperative, clarity of speech was crucial, but, most important of all, the *lectores* had to read the novels with their hearts.

Even the Spaniards were not able to extinguish the sacred union of words and smoke when they added their bloody chapter of infamy to history. In present-day Cuba, *lectores* still grace the cigar factories with their novels. In Tampa, the tradition came to an end at the beginning of the Depression. The introduction of machines to the cigar factories prohibited the listeners from fully surrendering their ears to the stories. Microphones were introduced to the workplace, but the necessary silence, which offers a stage for the spoken word, was missing. Finally, the *lectores* became seen as a threat to the factory owners, because of the labor press they were reading to the workers. The *lectores* were removed from the factories in 1931.

After writing *Anna in the Tropics* and presenting a series of readings of the script throughout the country, I was told by an audience member that he knew of a lector who read in a hat factory. The image of a lector surrounded by hat makers has stayed with me. Hats and words go together: what words would not want to enter a hat and somehow be close to the mind? I guess wedding gown factories would have been a good place for the *lectores* too, since the novels they read always spoke to the heart. I know that in my own humble way I've tried to give *lectores* a place in the theatre, so they can read aloud one more love story.

Nilo Cruz
September 2003

A version of this essay appeared in the L.A. Times, *September 28, 2003.*

AUTHOR'S NOTE

After 1931, the lectors were removed from the factories, and what remained of the cigar rollers consisted of low-paid American workers who operated machines. The end of a tradition.

Quotations from *Anna Karenina* by Leo Tolstoy:

"Looking at him"
Part 2, Chapter 11

"If there are as many minds"
Part 2, Chapter 7

"At first Anna sincerely thought"
Part 2, Chapter 4

"Anna had stepped into a new life"
Part 2, Chapter 11

"Anna Karenina's husband did not see anything peculiar"
Part 2, Chapter 8

"Anna Karenina prepared herself for the journey"
Part 1, Chapter 29

"In his youth, Anna Karenina's husband had been intrigued"
Part 3, Chapter 13

"By the time he arrived in Petersburg"
Part 3, Chapter 14

ANNA IN THE TROPICS was commissioned by New Theatre (Rafael de Acha, Artistic Director; Eileen Suarez, Managing Director) and received its world premiere in Coral Gables, Florida, on October 12, 2002. It was directed by Rafael de Acha; the set design was by Michelle Cumming; the lighting design was by Travis Neff; the original music and sound design were by M. Anthony Reimer; the costume design was by Estela Vrancovich; and the production stage manager was Margaret M. Ledford. The cast was as follows:

SANTIAGO .... Gonzalo Madurga
CHECHÉ .... Ken Clement
OFELIA .... Edna Schwab
MARELA .... Ursula Freundlich
CONCHITA .... Deborah L. Sherman
PALOMO .... Carlos Orizondo
JUAN JULIAN .... David Perez-Ribada
ELIADES .... Carlos Orizondo

ANNA IN THE TROPICS was subsequently developed and produced by the McCarter Theatre Center (Emily Mann, Artistic Director; Jeffrey Woodward, Managing Director). It opened in Princeton, New Jersey, on September 18, 2003. It was directed by Emily Mann; the set design was by Robert Brill; the lighting design was by Peter Kaczorowski; the sound design was by Dan Moses Schreier; the costume design was by Anita Yavich; and the production stage manager was Cheryl Mintz. The cast was as follows:

SANTIAGO .... Victor Argo
CHECHÉ .... David Zayas
OFELIA .... Priscilla Lopez
MARELA .... Vanessa Aspillaga
CONCHITA .... Daphne Rubin-Vega
PALOMO .... John Ortiz
JUAN JULIAN .... Jimmy Smits
ELIADES .... John Ortiz

This production transferred to the Royale Theatre on Broadway, opening on November 16, 2003. It was produced by Roger Berlind, Daryl Roth, Ray Larsen, in association with Robert Bartner.

CHARACTERS

SANTIAGO, owner of a cigar factory, late 50s

CHECHÉ, his half-brother; half-Cuban, half-American, early 40s

OFELIA, Santiago's wife, 50s

MARELA, Ofelia and Santiago's daughter, 22

CONCHITA, her sister, 32

PALOMO, her husband, 41

JUAN JULIAN, the lector, 38

ELIADES, local gamester, runs cockfights, 40s

PLACE

An old warehouse. Tampa, Florida. A small town called Ybor City.

TIME

1929.

COSTUMES

These workers are always well dressed. They use a lot of white and beige linen and their clothes are always well pressed and starched.

ANNA IN THE TROPICS

ACT ONE

Scene 1

*Sounds of a crowd at a cockfight. Santiago and Cheché are betting their money on cockfights. They've been drinking, but are not drunk. They wear typical, long-sleeve, white linen shirts (*guayabera*), white pants and two-tone shoes. Eliades collects the money and oversees all the operations of this place.*

ELIADES. Cockfights! See the winged beauties fighting in midair! Cockfights! I'll take five, ten, fifteen, twenty dollars on Picarubio. Five, ten, twenty on Espuela de Oro. Picarubio against Espuela de Oro. Espuela de Oro against Picarubio.

SANTIAGO. I'll bet a hundred on Picarubio.

ELIADES. A hundred on Picarubio.

CHECHÉ. Eighty on Espuela de Oro.

ELIADES. Eighty on Espuela de Oro.

SANTIAGO. Ten more on Picarubio.

ELIADES. Ten more on Picarubio. Ten more on Espuela de Oro?

CHECHÉ. No, that's enough.

ELIADES. I'll take five, ten, twenty dollars. Picarubio against Espuela de Oro. Espuela de Oro against Picarubio. *(Sound of a ship approaching the harbor. Marela, Conchita and their mother Ofelia are standing by the seaport. They are holding white handkerchiefs and are waiting for a ship to arrive.)*

MARELA. Is that the ship approaching in the distance?

CONCHITA. I think it is.

OFELIA. It's the only ship that's supposed to arrive around this time.

MARELA. Then that must be it. Oh, I'm so excited! Let me look at the picture again, Mamá.

OFELIA. How many times are you going to look at it?

MARELA. Many times. We have to make sure we know what he looks like.

CONCHITA. You just like looking at his face.

MARELA. I think he is elegant and good looking. *(Ofelia opens a letter and takes out a photograph.)*

OFELIA. That he is. But what's essential is that he has good vocal chords, deep lungs and a strong voice.

CONCHITA. What's more important is that he has good diction when he reads.

MARELA. As long as he reads with feeling and gusto, I'm content. *(Looks at the photo.)* Look at his face and the way he signs his name. *(Sounds of a crowd at a cockfight.)*

ELIADES. We have a winner! We have a winner! Espuela de Oro is the winner! Espuela de Oro!

CHECHÉ. Winner here.

ELIADES. *(Counting money.)* Ten, twenty, thirty, forty, fifty, sixty.

SANTIAGO. You're a lucky man.

ELIADES. Next fight! I'll take five, ten, fifteen, twenty dollars … Cuello de Jaca against Uñaroja. Uñaroja against Cuello de Jaca.

SANTIAGO. Eighty on Cuello de Jaca.

ELIADES. Eighty on Cuello de Jaca.

CHECHÉ. Eighty on Uñaroja.

ELIADES. Eighty on Uñaroja. *(To the audience.)* Uñaroja against Cuello de Jaca! Cuello de Jaca against Uñaroja! *(Sound of a ship approaching the harbor.)*

OFELIA. Don't tell your father, but I took some money from the safe to pay for the lector's trip.

CONCHITA. You did well, Mamá.

OFELIA. Oh, I don't feel a bit guilty. Doesn't your father spend his money gambling? Then I'll do as I wish with my money. I'll spend my money on the best lector we can get. The gentleman who recommended him says that he is the best lector west of Havana.

MARELA. Well, I'm glad, because poor old Teodoro used to spit a little too much when he read to us. Sometimes it felt like sprinkles of rain were coming out of his mouth.

OFELIA. Marela! The poor man was eighty years old.

MARELA. That he was!

OFELIA. Have more respect — he died three months ago.

MARELA. Oh, I respect him, but let the truth be told.

OFELIA. The poor fellow, for ten years he read to us.

MARELA. *(With satire.)* Oh, I loved him ... I loved him, like an uncle, like a grandfather. May he rest in peace! But he should've given up being a lector a long time ago. His heart couldn't take the love stories. He couldn't take the poetry and tragedy in the novels. Sometimes he had to sit down after reading a profound and romantic passage.

CONCHITA. Oh, that's why I liked him, because I knew that he read to us with his heart.

MARELA. But it was too much. It took him three months to read the last novel to us.

OFELIA. Ah! But it was *Wuthering Heights*, and none of us wanted it to end, including you.

CONCHITA. Well, I hope this new lector turns out to be as good as Teodoro, because the one who replaced him didn't last ...

MARELA. Look, the ship is getting closer. Oh, I'm so excited, I just want him to disembark and have him here once and for all.

CONCHITA. *(Looking into the distance.)* He's probably going to bring a lot of new books from Argentina and Spain and France, because so many ships make stops in Cuba. *(Sounds of a crowd at a cockfight.)*

ELIADES. We have a winner! We have a winner! Uñaroja! Uñaroja is the winner!

CHECHÉ. Winner here. Uñaroja. *(Eliades pays Cheché, then continues announcing the next fight.)*

ELIADES. Twenty, forty, sixty, eighty, one hundred ... Twenty, forty, sixty ... Ready for the next fight! We have Colabrava against Falcón de Acero. I'll take five, ten, fifteen, twenty dollars ... Colabrava against Falcón de Acero ... *(Continuing his announcement.)*

SANTIAGO. Lend me some money, Cheché.

CHECHÉ. How much?

SANTIAGO. Two hundred.

CHECHÉ. I don't lend any money when I'm gambling, and I don't lend any money when I'm drinking.

SANTIAGO. Are you going to make me walk home to get more money?

CHECHÉ. Ah, just give it up!

SANTIAGO. Are you going to make me walk back to my house?

CHECHÉ. It's not a good night for you! You've lost all your money.

SANTIAGO. Lend me some money, Cheché. I'll pay you back.

CHECHÉ. You're drunk, Santiago.

SANTIAGO. Give me some money and I'll show you my luck. Come on, you've got the lucky money! With your lucky money I'll show you what I can do.

CHECHÉ. And when are you going to pay me back?

SANTIAGO. I guarantee you that I'll pay you back.

CHECHÉ. You got to give me your word.

SANTIAGO. I'll give you my word. Give me a paper. I'll sign a paper. You got paper?

CHECHÉ. No, I don't have any paper.

SANTIAGO. Then lift up your foot.

CHECHÉ. What do you mean lift up my foot?

SANTIAGO *(Grabbing Cheché's leg.)* Lift up your foot, hombre!

CHECHÉ. What the hell? …

SANTIAGO. Let me have the sole of your shoe. *(Santiago takes out a knife.)*

CHECHÉ. What are you going to do? *(Lifting up his foot.)*

SANTIAGO. I'm signing my name on the sole of your shoe. *(Santiago carves his name on Cheché's shoe.)*

CHECHÉ. What for?

SANTIAGO. Proof. Testament that I'll pay you back. See here: "S" for Santiago. How much are you going to lend me?

CHECHÉ. Twenty.

SANTIAGO. Twenty? Cheapskate. I'm writing a hundred.

CHECHÉ. A hundred?

SANTIAGO. A hundred. There you go.

CHECHÉ. A hundred?

SANTIAGO. A hundred. That's what I wrote.

CHECHÉ. Are you…?

SANTIAGO. I'll pay you back. I'm your brother, for God's sake! *(Sound of a ship approaching the harbor.)*

OFELIA. There is the ship. Wave your handkerchief.

MARELA. Do you see him?

CONCHITA. All the men look the same with their hats.

OFELIA. Oh, why do I get so emotional every time I see a ship?

MARELA. Don't get mad at me, Mamá, but I wrote the lector's name on a piece of paper and placed it in a glass of water with brown sugar and cinnamon.

OFELIA. What for?

MARELA. Carmela, the palm reader, told me that if I sweeten his name, the reader would come our way.

OFELIA. That's like casting a spell on him.

MARELA. It's only sugar and cinnamon. And it worked.

OFELIA. I told you about playing with spells. It's not right, Marela. One should never alter other people's destiny.

MARELA. I didn't alter his destiny. With a little sugar I sweetened his fate.

CONCHITA. That's how witches get started — with brown sugar. Then they begin to play with fire. Look at what happened to Rosario, she put a spell on her lover and the man died. And not only did she lose her man; she's gone to hell herself.

OFELIA. *(To Marela.)* Did you hear that?

CONCHITA. They say she couldn't stop crying after her lover's death. That her whole face became an ocean of tears, and the father had to take her back to Cuba, to see if she would get better. But a fever would possess the girl at night. They say she'd run to the sea naked. She'd run there to meet the dead lover.

MARELA. Now you're making me feel awful. *(Sounds of a crowd at a cockfight.)*

ELIADES. Kikiriki ... Ready for the next fight! We have Diamante Negro against Crestafuerte ... I'll take five, ten, fifteen, twenty dollars ... Diamante Negro against Crestafuerte. Crestafuerte against Diamante Negro.

SANTIAGO. Lift up your foot again.

CHECHÉ. What for?

SANTIAGO. Lift up your foot and let me see the sole of your shoe.

CHECHÉ. What for? *(Santiago carves something on the sole of Cheché's shoe.)*

SANTIAGO. I'm borrowing two hundred more.

CHECHÉ. No. You can't. You're jinxed tonight.

SANTIAGO. I'll pay you back. It's written on your shoe already.

CHECHÉ. Then cross it out.

SANTIAGO. I can't cross it out. I've got my totals there. If I don't pay you, part of the factory is yours. *(Immediately Cheché takes off his shoe.)*

CHECHÉ. Then write it down. Write it down. I want it in writing.

SANTIAGO. I'll write it down. *(Takes the knife and carves out his promise.)* There you go. *(Cheché looks at the sole of his shoe. He gives Santiago more money.)*

CHECHÉ. Here. Let's go.

SANTIAGO. Well, put on your shoe, hombre!

CHECHÉ. No, I'm not putting it on.

17

SANTIAGO. Why not?

CHECHÉ. Because this here is our contract, and I don't want it erased.

SANTIAGO. And you're going to walk with just one shoe.

CHECHÉ. Yes!

SANTIAGO. You bastard! *(Sound of a ship approaching.)*

OFELIA. Well, there's no sign of him. Let's see if you spoiled it for us.

MARELA. Ah, don't say that! I'm so nervous I think I'm going to pee-pee on myself.

CONCHITA. Is he that man waving his hat?

OFELIA. Is it? I can't see very well from here.

CONCHITA. No. He's got to be younger.

MARELA. How is he going to recognize us?

OFELIA. I told him that I was going to wear a white hat.

MARELA. Oh Lord! There are more than fifty women with white hats.

OFELIA. But I told him that my hat would have a gardenia.

CONCHITA. Is it the man with the blue suit?

MARELA. No, too fat.

OFELIA. When you get home take his name out of that sweet water.

MARELA. Oh Lord, I feel awful. He's nowhere to be found. I'm going home. I'm going home. I've ruined it. *(Starts to exit.)*

OFELIA. Marela!

MARELA. No. I've ruined it.

OFELIA. Come back here. A little bit of sugar can't do any harm. *(The lector, Juan Julian, enters. He is wearing a Panama hat and a white linen suit.)*

MARELA. I don't want to spoil it.

OFELIA. Marela, don't be foolish.

JUAN JULIAN. Señora Ofelia?

OFELIA. *(Turning to look.)* Yes …

JUAN JULIAN. The gardenia on your hat, am I correct? Señora Ofelia. *(Juan Julian takes off his hat.)*

OFELIA. *(Dumbstruck.)* Oh!

CONCHITA. Say yes, Mamá!

OFELIA. Ah, yes! I'm Ofelia.

JUAN JULIAN. Juan Julian Rios, at your service!

OFELIA. Ah! Ofelia … Ofelia Alcalar. What an honor! *(We hear Marela pee on herself from nervousness. There is an awkward pause. All of them notice. Dissimulating.)* Oh! Do you have everything,

Señor Juan Julian? Do you have your luggage?

JUAN JULIAN: I'll have to tell the steward that I found you.

OFELIA. Go find him ... We'll wait here. *(Juan Julian runs off. Turning to Marela.)* Marela, what happened?

MARELA. *(Dumbstruck.)* I don't know.

OFELIA. Oh dear! But you've wet yourself, like a child.

MARELA. I couldn't hold it in, Mamá. *(Music plays. Lights change.)*

Scene 2

The cigar factory. Juan Julian is holding a few books strapped with a belt. Cheché enters. He wears one shoe and holds the other in his hand.

CHECHÉ. Are you here to see someone?

JUAN JULIAN. I'm here to see Ofelia.

CHECHÉ. Ofelia hasn't come yet. Can I help you?

JUAN JULIAN. She told me she'd be here around this time.

CHECHÉ. She should be getting here soon. Can I be of any service?

JUAN JULIAN. No, thank you. I'll wait.

CHECHÉ. What are you, a lector?

JUAN JULIAN. Yes, I am. I just arrived from the island. Today is my first day ...

CHECHÉ. If you're looking for a job, we're not hiring ...

JUAN JULIAN. No, I'm ... I'm the new lector. Doña Ofelia —

CHECHÉ. I heard. You just arrived and I'm telling you we're not hiring ...

JUAN JULIAN. Well, I imagine you are not hiring because Señora Ofelia ... *(Ofelia and her daughters enter.)*

CHECHÉ. Ofelia, the señor ... this gentleman is here to see you. I told him we're not hiring ...

OFELIA. *(With conviction.)* He's been hired by me, Chester.

CHECHÉ. Oh, I see. I see. *(Pause.)* Oh, well. *(Cheché exits.)*

OFELIA. Welcome, Juan Julian. Some of the cigar rollers who work in front told me they already met you. They're very excited that you're here.

JUAN JULIAN. Ah yes. I was talking to the gentleman wearing the fedora who sits all the way to the right.

OFELIA. Peppino Mellini. He's the best buncher we have. He is from Napoli. He has a soft spot for the love stories. He is the one that sings Neapolitan songs at the end of the day.

JUAN JULIAN. And I also met Palomo, the gentleman with the Panama hat.

CONCHITA. My husband. He is a roller like us.

OFELIA. And did you meet Manola?

JUAN JULIAN. Is she the lady with the picture of Valentino on top of her table?

OFELIA. Yes, she does the stuffing. Oh, she's delighted that you are here. Sometimes she's a sea of tears when she listens to the stories.

JUAN JULIAN. And the gentleman with the handkerchief around his neck?

OFELIA. Ah, that's Pascual Torino from Spain. He does the wrapping. A nostalgic at heart, wants to go back to his country and die in Granada.

JUAN JULIAN. And the gentleman that was just here?

MARELA. Chester is a clown. *(Conchita and Marela laugh.)*

OFELIA. Marela! We call him Cheché. He is my husband's half-brother. We didn't know he was part of the family, but one day he showed up at the factory with a birth certificate and said he was my father-in-law's son. So we took him in, and ever since, he's been part of the family. But he is really from a town up north. *(Laughs.)* My father-in-law got around.

JUAN JULIAN. I think that my presence offends him.

MARELA. Oh, that can't be. Don't pay him any mind.

JUAN JULIAN. When I entered the factory this morning he turned his back on me and then he ...

MARELA. Cheché thinks he owns the factory. *(Breaks into laughter.)*

OFELIA. My husband has given him a little too much power. But it's my husband who really runs the factory.

CONCHITA. Don't mind him. Cheché has a knack for turning the smallest incident into a loud and tragic event.

JUAN JULIAN. But I didn't do anything to the man.

MARELA. He doesn't like lectors.

OFELIA. He doesn't understand the purpose of having someone like you read stories to the workers.

JUAN JULIAN. But that has always been the tradition.

CONCHITA. He's from another culture.

MARELA. He thinks that lectors are the ones who cause trouble.

JUAN JULIAN. Why? Because we read novels to the workers, because we educate them and inform them?

MARELA. No. It's more complicated than that. His wife ran away from home with a lector.

OFELIA. Marela! He doesn't need to know these things!

MARELA. But it's true. She disappeared one day with the lector that was working here. She was a southern belle from Atlanta and he was from Guanabacoa. Her skin was pale like a lily and he was the color of saffron.

And of course, now Cheché is against all lectors and the love stories they read.

JUAN JULIAN. But he can't put the blame …

MARELA. Cheché thinks the love stories got under her skin. That's why she left him.

OFELIA. That's enough, Marela! When all this happened the poor man was desperate, angry and sad. He couldn't accept reality, so he blamed the lectors and the love stories for his misfortune.

CONCHITA. If he's ever disrespectful you should talk to our father.

OFELIA. Don't you worry. I'll take care of him.

MARELA. What are you planning to read to us?

JUAN JULIAN. First, Tolstoy, *Anna Karenina*.

MARELA. *Anna Karenina*. I already like the title. Is it romantic?

JUAN JULIAN. Yes. Quite romantic.

MARELA. Ah, *Anna Karenina* will go right to Cheché's heart. The poor man. He won't be able to take it.

JUAN JULIAN. I could pick another book. I've brought many.

CONCHITA. No, read *Anna Karenina* if that's the book that you chose.

MARELA. He needs to listen to another love story and let the words make nests in his hair, so he can find another woman.

OFELIA. And how do you like Tampa so far, Juan Julian?

JUAN JULIAN. Well, I … I … It's very … It seems like it's a city in the making.

OFELIA. That it is. We are still trying to create a little city that resembles the ones we left back in the island.

JUAN JULIAN. It's curious, there are no mountains or hills here. Lots of sky I have noticed … And clouds … The largest clouds I've ever seen, as if they had soaked up the whole sea. It's all so flat all around. That's why the sky seems so much bigger here and infinite.

Bigger than the sky I know back home. And there's so much light. There doesn't seem to be a place where one could hide.

MARELA. One can always find shade in the park. There's always a hiding place to be found, and if not, one can always hide behind light.

JUAN JULIAN. Really. And how does one hide behind light? *(The women laugh nervously.)*

MARELA. Depends what you are hiding from.

JUAN JULIAN. Perhaps light itself.

MARELA. Well, there are many kinds of light. The light of fires. The light of stars. The light that reflects off rivers. Light that penetrates through cracks. Then there's the type of light that reflects off the skin. Which one?

JUAN JULIAN. Perhaps the type that reflects off the skin.

MARELA. That's the most difficult one to escape. *(The women laugh. Cheché enters. He is still holding the shoe in his hand.)*

CHECHÉ. Ofelia, why didn't Santiago come to work today?

OFELIA. He went to Camacho's house. Is there a problem, Cheché?

CHECHÉ. No, I'd just like to talk about ... Will he come by later?

OFELIA. I don't know. What's wrong with your foot?

CHECHÉ. Oh, it's a long story. You see ... I ...

OFELIA. Did you fall? Did you hurt yourself?

CHECHÉ. No. I ... It's nothing.

OFELIA. I know my feet are worse each day. If it isn't a bunion hurting, it's an ingrown nail.

CHECHÉ. No, Ofelia. Nothing of the sort.

OFELIA. Then why are you walking...?

CHECHÉ. Well, you see ... My shoes for work ... I ... I took them to the shoemaker yesterday and they weren't ready today.

OFELIA. So, these are new shoes and they hurt your feet.

CHECHÉ. No, you see ... I mean ... Last night Santiago and I ... We ... You see, we went to the cockfights.

OFELIA. Ha! That explains it. You lost all your money and your shoes.

CHECHÉ. No, I didn't lose my money. Your husband lost all his money and some of mine. *(Ofelia laughs.)*

OFELIA. So are you giving me this shoe so I can throw it at him and break his head? *(The women laugh.)*

CHECHÉ. No, Ofelia ... I ...

OFELIA. So what's with the shoe? Are you collecting alms?

Instead of passing the bucket or the hat are you passing the shoe?

CHECHÉ. Well, I'm sort of passing it to you.

OFELIA. I don't have any money, Cheché.

CHECHÉ. I'm not asking you for money. *(Juan Julian and the sisters exit.)*

OFELIA. Then why are you pointing this thing at me?

CHECHÉ. You see here. Right here, on the sole of my shoe, Santiago wrote how much he owes me.

OFELIA. And how much does he owe you?

CHECHÉ. The total is here. *(Ofelia looks at the shoe.)*

OFELIA. That's a lot of money.

CHECHÉ. That's how much he owes me.

OFELIA. Where did you get so much money?

CHECHÉ. I was winning.

OFELIA. And you drank and gave it all away.

CHECHÉ. No. I ... Well, he wanted to continue playing. He didn't want to walk home to get more money, so I lent him what I had. And he told me he'd sign my shoe and write the totals. And I trust that he'll pay me back.

OFELIA. So what do you want me to do?

CHECHÉ. Well, this here is a bill. A document.

OFELIA. You're not serious!

CHECHÉ. No. This here is an agreement. If he doesn't pay me ... You see here. You see his initials ... He signed this! He signed it! He told me that if he didn't pay me, another share of the factory would be mine.

OFELIA. Get this thing out of my sight.

CHECHÉ. But Ofelia ...

OFELIA. Get it out my sight, I said.

CHECHÉ. But Ofelia ...

OFELIA. I don't know what went on between you and your brother, but I don't have anything to do with it. And you better go to a shoemaker and get your shoes mended. *(Music plays. Lights change.)*

Scene 3

Juan Julian strides around the cigar workers reading from Tolstoy's Anna Karenina. *He reads with passion and fervor. The cigar workers roll, but are completely immersed in the story.*

JUAN JULIAN. *(Reading.)* "Looking at him, Anna Karenina felt a physical humiliation and could not say another word. Her beloved felt what a killer must feel when he looks at the body he has deprived of life. The body he had deprived of life was their love, the beginning of their love. There was something dreadful and revolting in the recollection of what had been paid for by this awful price of shame. The shame Anna sensed from their spiritual nakedness destroyed her and affected him. But in spite of the killer's horror when he faces the body of his victim, the killer must cut the body to pieces and conceal it, and he must make use of what he has gained by his crime. And with the same fury and passion as the killer throws himself upon the body and drags it and cuts it, he covered her face and shoulders with kisses. 'Yes, these kisses — these kisses are what have been bought by my shame.'" *(Juan Julian closes the book.)* That's all for today from *Anna Karenina. (The workers applaud.)*

MARELA. *(Still enraptured by the story.)* Why does he always end when he gets to the good part?

OFELIA. To keep us in suspense.

CONCHITA. To keep us wanting more.

MARELA. He's really a fine lector.

OFELIA. That's why he's called the Persian Canary, because it's like hearing a bird sing when he reads.

MARELA. And can you smell the cologne from his handkerchief every time he dries his forehead? The fragrance wraps itself around the words like smoke.

CHECHÉ. *(To Palomo.)* Oh Lord! Exactly what I expected. Now they'll sigh and chat about the love story for hours.

MARELA. I heard that, Cheché.

CHECHÉ. Oh, but this is the part I like the most, when you start discussing things. For some reason I never hear the story the same way that you do.

PALOMO. Neither do I, but maybe that's because we're men.

MARELA. You're being cynical.

CONCHITA. Don't pay them any mind.

PALOMO. No. I'd like to hear what you have to say.

CONCHITA. Mamá, you did well in sending for him.

OFELIA. Only a fool can fail to understand the importance of having a lector read to us while we work.

MARELA. Well, Cheché is not very happy with him.

OFELIA. That's because Cheché is a fool.

CHECHÉ. Now I haven't said —

OFELIA. I heard what you told Palomo this morning and we're not going to do away with the lector.

CHECHÉ. All I said —

OFELIA. When I lived in Havana I don't remember ever seeing a tobacco factory without a lector. As a child I remember sitting in the back and listening to the stories. That has always been our pride. Some of us cigar workers might not be able to read or write, but we can recite lines from *Don Quixote* or *Jane Eyre*.

CHECHÉ. All I said was that I'm afraid we're in for another tragic love story.

PALOMO. I like love stories.

MARELA. Me, too.

CHECHÉ. I would've preferred a detective story.

MARELA. They're not very literary, Chester.

CONCHITA. Well. I don't know about you, but ever since he started reading *Anna Karenina* my mind wanders to Russia.

MARELA. Me, too. I have dreams and they are full of white snow, and Anna Karenina is dancing waltzes with Vronsky. Then I see them in a little room, and all the snow melts from the heat of their bodies and their skin. And I just want to borrow a fur coat from my friend Cookie Salazar and go to Russia.

OFELIA. He chose the right book. There is nothing like reading a winter book in the middle of summer. It's like having a fan or an icebox by your side to relieve the heat and the caloric nights.

CHECHÉ. *(To Palomo.)* Help me with the boxes. *(The men exit.)*

MARELA. What was that last line? "And, as with fury and passion the killer throws himself upon … "

CONCHITA. "Upon the body," he said, "and drags it and cuts it, he covered her face and shoulders with kisses."

MARELA. Does it mean that when you're in love your body is stolen from life?

CONCHITA. No. The body robbed of life was their love. The love of Anna and her beloved.

OFELIA. It must be terrible living that way.

MARELA. Why?

OFELIA. How the three of them live! Anna, the husband and the lover. It must be a nightmare.

MARELA. Of course not! *(Conchita refers to the story, but also to her own life.)*

CONCHITA. Yes. Anna said it herself. It's like a curse, she said. She was talking about it at the end, when she said that his kisses have been bought by her shame. She's got to be miserable.

MARELA. Miserable? Enraptured maybe.

OFELIA. You don't listen to the story, Marela.

MARELA. Of course I listen to the story.

CONCHITA. Then you ought to know that it is misery for her. It's pure agony for Anna's husband and for the lover, too. They probably couldn't endure it any longer, if it weren't for some kind of hope.

MARELA. Then why would she take on a lover?

OFELIA. She has no choice. It's something she can't escape. That's why the writer describes love as a thief. The thief is the mysterious fever that poets have been studying for years. Remember Anna Karenina's last words.

CONCHITA. She never remembers anything.

MARELA. I do. I just don't cling to every word the way you do. I don't try to understand everything they say. I let myself be taken. When Juan Julian starts reading, the story enters my body and I become the second skin of the characters.

OFELIA. Don't be silly.

MARELA. We can always dream.

OFELIA. Ah yes. But we have to take a yardstick and measure our dreams.

MARELA. Then I will need a very long yardstick. The kind that could measure the sky.

CONCHITA. How foolish you are, Marela!

MARELA. *(To Conchita.)* No, everything in life dreams. A bicycle dreams of becoming a boy, an umbrella dreams of becoming the rain, a pearl dreams of becoming a woman, and a chair dreams of becoming a gazelle and running back to the forest.

OFELIA. But, my child, people like us ... We have to remember to keep our feet on the ground and stay living inside our shoes and not

have lofty illusions. *(A bell rings. Palomo enters.)* Ah, workday has come to an end. Good. I rolled more than two hundred cigars today.
MARELA. And I've wedded more than a thousand. That's what I like about putting the bands around the cigars. It's like marrying all these men without actually seeing them.
OFELIA. Men marry their cigars, my dear, and the white smoke becomes the veil of their brides. My mother used to say, "When a man marries, he marries two women, his bride and his cigar." Are you coming, Conchita?
CONCHITA. No. Palomo and I are working till late.
OFELIA. We'll see you for dinner. Adios.
CONCHITA. Adios.
OFELIA. Till later, Palomo.
PALOMO. Adios.
MARELA. Adios.
PALOMO. Is your father in trouble again and that's why...?
CONCHITA. He is.
PALOMO. How much did he lose this time?
CONCHITA. Plenty.
PALOMO. Plenty can be a lot of money.
CONCHITA. Yes, you're right. And I don't know what good he gets from losing all that money.
PALOMO. Oh, that's something we'll never know. *(Beginning to roll.)*
CONCHITA. And how do you like the novel that Juan Julian is reading to us?
PALOMO. I like it very much.
CONCHITA. Doesn't it make you uncomfortable?
PALOMO. Why would it make me uncomfortable?
CONCHITA. The part about the lover.
PALOMO. It seems like in every novel there's always a love affair.
CONCHITA. And do you ever think about everything that's happening between Anna Karenina and her husband?
PALOMO. I do ... But I ...
CONCHITA. So what goes through your mind when you listen to the story?
PALOMO. I think of the money all those people have.
CONCHITA. You would say something like that.
PALOMO. Why? Because I like money?
CONCHITA. I'm talking about literature and you talk about money.

PALOMO. And what do you want me to say?

CONCHITA. I want you to talk about the story, the characters ...

PALOMO. Wouldn't you like to have all the money they have? So you don't have to spend the whole day rolling cigars and working after hours so we can save money and have our own business.

CONCHITA. I don't mind rolling cigars.

PALOMO. And what's so good about rolling cigars?

CONCHITA. My mind wanders to other places.

PALOMO. What places?

CONCHITA. Places and things money can't buy.

PALOMO. Money can buy everything.

CONCHITA. Not the places I go to in my mind.

PALOMO. And what kind of places are you talking about?

CONCHITA. Places made of dreams.

PALOMO. *(Laughs; becoming playful.)* You're a strange creature, Conchita. I don't know why I married you.

CONCHITA. You married me because the day you met me, I gave you a cigar I had rolled especially for you and when you smoked it, you told me I had slipped into your mouth like a pearl diver.

PALOMO. I told you that?

CONCHITA. Yes, you did. After blowing a blue ring of smoke out of your mouth. And the words lingered in the air like a zeppelin and I thought to myself, I could fall in love with that mouth.

PALOMO. As far as I can remember, I married you because I couldn't untie your father's hands from around my neck.

CONCHITA. Ah, the truth comes out. That explains everything. You never really cared for me.

PALOMO. Are you trying to start a fight?

CONCHITA. No. I asked you a simple question about a love story and you're being foolish.

PALOMO. Never mind.

CONCHITA. You don't care about anything, do you? Juan Julian could be reading a book by José Martí or Shakespeare and everything goes in one ear and out the other.

PALOMO. I pay attention to what he reads.

I just don't take everything to heart the way you do.

CONCHITA. Well, you should. Do you remember that part of the book in which Anna Karenina's husband is suspicious of her having an affair with Vronsky? Remember when he paces the room, like a lost animal.

PALOMO. I know what you're getting at.

CONCHITA. I just want to have a civilized conversation. The same way the characters speak to each other in the novel. I've learned many things from this book.

PALOMO. Such as?

CONCHITA. Jealousy. For Anna's husband jealousy is base and almost animalistic. And he's right. He would never want Anna to think that he's capable of such vile and shameful emotions.

PALOMO. But you can't help being jealous. It's part of your nature.

CONCHITA. Not anymore.

PALOMO. Well, that's a change.

CONCHITA. Oh, I could see the husband so clear in the novel. How the thoughts would take shape in his mind, as they have in my own mind. I mean, not the same ... No, no ... Not the same, because he's an educated man, surrounded by culture and wealth, and I'm just a cigar roller in a factory. He is well bred and sophisticated. I barely get by in life.

But with this book I'm seeing everything through new eyes. What is happening in the novel has been happening to us.

No. Don't look at me that way. You might not want to admit it, but Anna and her husband remind me of us. Except I'm more like the husband.

PALOMO. So what does that make me then, Anna Karenina?

CONCHITA. You are the one who has the secret love, not me.

PALOMO. Oh, come on. It's late. Let's go home. I can't work like this.

CONCHITA. That's exactly what Anna said when the husband confronted her about the lover: "It's late. Let's go to sleep."

PALOMO. I think you're taking this a little too far.

CONCHITA. Am I? Have you ever heard the voice of someone who's deaf? The voice is crude and ancient, because it has no sense of direction or place, because it doesn't hear itself and it doesn't know if anybody else in the world hears it. Sometimes I want to have a long conversation with you, like this. Like a deaf person. As if I couldn't hear you or myself. But I would just talk and talk, and say everything that comes to my mind, like a shell that shouts with the voice of the sea and it doesn't care if anybody ever hears it. That's how I want to speak to you, and ask you things.

PALOMO. And what's the use of talking like this? What sort of things do you want to ask me?

CONCHITA. Things that you wouldn't tell me, afraid that I might not understand.

PALOMO. Like what?

CONCHITA. I'd like to know what she's like. And what does she do to make you happy?

PALOMO. Ah, let's go home.

CONCHITA. Why?

PALOMO. *(Abruptly.)* Because I don't want to talk about these things! *(A pause.)*

CONCHITA. So what's going to happen to us, Palomo?

PALOMO. I don't know. Do you want a divorce? We could travel to Reno and be divorced in six weeks. But your family will be opposed to it, and the same with mine. So divorce is out of the question.

CONCHITA. And if I tell you that I want to cut my hair, change the way I dress and take on a lover.

PALOMO. Say that again?

CONCHITA. What I just said.

PALOMO. You want to have a lover?

CONCHITA. Yes, like you do.

PALOMO. Ave Maria purissima!

CONCHITA. I have the same right as you do.

PALOMO. This book will be the end of us.

CONCHITA. Don't you think we've already come to the end?

PALOMO. No ... I ...

CONCHITA. You don't make love to me like you used to.

PALOMO. Well, we ... You and I ... We ...

CONCHITA. It's all right, Palomo. It's all right. *(She touches his arm.)* There's something that Anna Karenina said and I keep repeating it to myself: "If there are as many minds as there are heads, then there are as many kinds of love as there are hearts." I can try to love you in a different way. I can do that. And you should try to do the same. *(Music plays. Lights change.)*

Scene 4

A square of light on the floor suggests the interior of the family's house. Ofelia and Santiago are not on speaking terms. She sits on one side of the room, he sits on the other. Marela stands by Santiago. The dialogue moves fast. Marela runs back and forth as a communicator.

SANTIAGO. Ask your mother for some money to buy me a pack of cigarettes. She's not talking to me.

MARELA. Papá wants money for a pack of cigarettes.

OFELIA. Ask him when is he going back to work.

MARELA. She wants to know when you're going back to work.

SANTIAGO. Tell her as soon as I get money from Camacho to pay Cheché.

MARELA. He says as soon as he gets money from Camacho to pay Cheché.

OFELIA. Tell him to give up smoking till then, that I'm not giving him any money.

SANTIAGO. What did she say?

MARELA. She says —

SANTIAGO. I heard her. *(In loud voice, to Ofelia.)* Tell her that she's insane!

MARELA. He says you're insane.

OFELIA. And tell him he's a drunk, a thief and a good-for-nothing gambler.

MARELA. She says —

SANTIAGO. I heard.

MARELA. He heard you, Mamá.

OFELIA. Good!

MARELA. Good, she says.

SANTIAGO. You're a crazy woman! Crazy woman!

OFELIA. Tell him I didn't hear that. I told him I don't want him to talk to me.

SANTIAGO. Ah, she heard me!

OFELIA. Tell him I don't want to hear his barbarisms.

MARELA. Did you hear that, Papá? She doesn't want to hear your barbarisms.

SANTIAGO. Tell her ... *(Marela starts to walk toward her father.)*

OFELIA. *(Infuriated.)* Come here, Marela ... *(Marela walks toward her mother.)*

SANTIAGO. Marela, come here ...

MARELA. Wait! It's not your turn, Mamá.

OFELIA. Marela ...

MARELA. Stop! I can't be here and there at the same time! *(Silence. Ofelia and Santiago shake their heads as if giving up on the whole thing.)*

OFELIA and SANTIAGO. This is insane!

MARELA. Well, you both heard that. *(Marela tries to put in a word, but they don't give her a chance.)*

SANTIAGO. Tell her I'm going to a pawnshop to sell my wedding ring.

OFELIA. Tell him he should've done that a long time ago.

SANTIAGO. She's right, I should've done it a long time ago.

OFELIA. Yes, before his finger got numb.

SANTIAGO. She's right, my finger got numb.

OFELIA. You see, I was right. Numb, like everything else.

SANTIAGO. She's wrong. Not like everything else.

OFELIA. Nothing works on his body. Just his rotten teeth to chew away money.

MARELA. I'm leaving.

OFELIA. Marela!

SANTIAGO. Marela!

MARELA. You can fight without me! *(Marela walks out of the room. Silence. Then, Ofelia and Santiago begin to speak to each other without looking at each other.)*

SANTIAGO. I've been listening to the new lector from up here.

OFELIA. You have?

SANTIAGO. He's good. He has a solid voice and I like the novel that he's reading.

OFELIA. Yes, a solid voice he has and I like the novel, too.

SANTIAGO. I 'specially like the character that lives in the country-side.

OFELIA. *(With delight.)* Yes.

SANTIAGO. Yes, him.

OFELIA. The one that has the farm?

SANTIAGO. Yes. The one that has the farm. What is his name?

OFELIA. His name is Levin.

SANTIAGO. That's right, Levin.

OFELIA. The one that lives in the forest surrounded by trees.

SANTIAGO. That Levin reminds me of when I was young and my father left me to run the factory. It seems as if Levin has dedicated his whole life to his farm.

OFELIA. Yes, he's a dedicated man.

SANTIAGO. I used to be like him.

OFELIA. Yes, you used to be like him.

SANTIAGO. I like the part of the book when Anna's brother is going to sell the estate next to Levin's property and Levin counsels him not to sell it.

OFELIA. Yes, that's a good part. And I can't believe that you almost gave another share of the factory to Cheché.

SANTIAGO. You're right, I lost my mind. I shouldn't drink.

OFELIA. That's right, drink you shouldn't. That's an idiotic thing to do, give away another share of the business. Cheché doesn't know what he's doing. He's like a scarecrow. He's been talking about bringing machines and replacing some of the workers. You need to go back to the factory.

SANTIAGO. Yes, you're right. To the factory I need to go back. *(Ofelia looks at him.)*

OFELIA. Santiago, what's eating you? You haven't gone to work. You don't eat. You don't sleep well.

SANTIAGO. I've acted like a fool, Ofelia. I'm ashamed of myself and I'm angry and bitter. And I can't shake off this damn agony!

OFELIA. Do you want me to call a doctor?

SANTIAGO. No. I don't need a doctor.

OFELIA. But you can't go on like this. Sooner or later you have to go back and face the workers.

SANTIAGO. I will. When I get the money and I can face Cheché.

OFELIA. And are you going to stay here until then?

SANTIAGO. Yes.

OFELIA. That's silly.

SANTIAGO. That's the way I am.

OFELIA. Well, I'm going to bed. *(Ofelia starts to exit.)*

SANTIAGO. Ofelia.

OFELIA. Yes.

SANTIAGO. Stay up a while longer.

OFELIA. I'm tired. You didn't work like I did today.

SANTIAGO. Talk to me about the novel. I can't always hear very well from up here. This fellow, Levin … This character that I admire ... He's the one who is in love with the young girl in the story, isn't he?

OFELIA. *(A burst of energy.)* Ah yes! He's in love with Kitty. Levin is in love with Kitty, and Kitty is in love with Vronsky. And Vronsky is in love with Anna Karenina. And Anna Karenina is married, but she's in love with Vronsky. Ay, everybody is in love in this book!

SANTIAGO. But for Levin ... For Levin there's only one woman.

OFELIA. Yes, for him there's only one woman.

SANTIAGO. *(Full of love, he looks at her.)* Ofelia.

OFELIA. Yes. *(Santiago swallows the gulp of love.)*

SANTIAGO. No. Nothing.

OFELIA. *(Fanning herself.)* Ah, the night breeze is making its way to us again. There's nothing like this Tampa breeze, always a punctual visitor around this time.

SANTIAGO. You know, Ofelia, when I gamble I try to repeat the same motions ... I try to repeat everything I did the day I won. And when I lose I try to take inventory of what I did wrong. I think to myself, Did I get up from bed with my left foot first? Did I forget to polish my shoes? Did I leave the house in a state of disorder? Was I unkind to someone and that's why luck didn't come my way? Lately, I've been in a fog and I don't know what to do.

Every time I lose, I feel that something has been taken from me. Something bigger than money. And I see a line of little ants carrying breadcrumbs on their backs. But the crumbs they are taking away are my pride and my self-respect. My dignity. *(Looks at her again.)* Have I lost you too, Ofelia? Have I lost you?

OFELIA. If you had lost me, I wouldn't be here. If you had lost me, I wouldn't be by your side. How can you say that you've lost me! *(She hugs him. Music plays. Lights change.)*

Scene 5

Juan Julian, Marela and Conchita at the factory.

JUAN JULIAN. I don't really like cities. In the country one has freedom. When I'm in a city I feel asphyxiated. I feel constriction in my lungs. The air feels thick and dense, as if the buildings

34

breathe and steal away the oxygen. As my father used to say, living in a city is like living inside the mouth of a crocodile, buildings all around you like teeth. The teeth of culture, the mouth and tongue of civilization. It's a silly comparison, but it makes sense to me.

Every time I go to a park, I'm reminded of how we always go back to nature. We build streets and buildings. We work five to six days a week, building and cementing our paths and down come tumbling trees and nests, a whole paradise of insects. And all for what? On Sundays we return to a park where we could still find greenery. The verdure of nature.

CONCHITA. You're right. I don't know what I would do without my walks to the park. Why did you choose to read Tolstoy?

JUAN JULIAN. Because Tolstoy understands humanity like no other writer does.

CONCHITA. That's a good enough reason to read him.

JUAN JULIAN. Someone told me that at the end of his life, when he knew he was going to die, he abandoned his house and he was found dead at a train station. The same as …

Oh, perhaps I shouldn't tell you this.

CONCHITA. He was probably on his way to visit God.

JUAN JULIAN. That has always been my suspicion.

MARELA. Pardon me, but I must go. *(She exits. There is an awkward pause as Juan Julian and Conchita watch Marela leave.)*

CONCHITA. How did you become a lector?

JUAN JULIAN. I discovered books one summer. My father owed a lot of money to a creditor and we had to close ourselves up in our house and hide for a while. For my family, keeping up appearances was important. We had to pretend that we had gone away on a trip. We told neighbors that my mother was ill and she had to recuperate somewhere else. We stayed in that closed-up house for more than two months, while my father worked abroad. I remember it was hot and all the windows were kept closed. The heat was unbearable. The maid was the only one who went out to buy groceries. And while being closed up in our own home my mother read books to the family. And that's when I became a listener and I learned to appreciate stories and the sound of words. *(Smiles.)* Have you ever been to New England?

CONCHITA. No.

JUAN JULIAN. I always wanted to go there. I wonder what New Englanders are like. Here I have met workers from other parts of the world, but I haven't met anybody from up North.

CONCHITA. Cheché is from up North.

JUAN JULIAN. Cheché is from a world of his own.

CONCHITA. I knew a fellow from New London. He was modest and reserved. So shy was this boy, that when he expressed any sort of feeling, he would excuse himself. *(Laughs.)* One day I gave him a braid that I'd cut from my hair and told him to bury it under a tree. I explained to him that back in the island most women cut their hair once a year on the second of February, when plants and trees are pruned, for the feast of Saint Candelaria. I told him how women offer their hair to the earth and the trees, for all the greenery and fruits to come. And I gave him my little braid in a box and told him to choose a tree in the park.

And the boy looked at me with a strange face and said that he would feel embarrassed digging a hole in the middle of the park, in front of everybody. And that's when I took my braid back from him, took a shovel, dug a hole and put him to shame. From then on he never talked to me again. So he's the only person from New England that I've met. *(Palomo enters. He watches from a distance.)*

JUAN JULIAN. *(Laughs.)* And do you still cut your hair every second of February?

CONCHITA. Yes. My father always does me the honor of burying it.

JUAN JULIAN. Your father! And why not your husband? It should be an honor for any man ... If I were your husband I would find an old, wise, banyan tree and I would bury your hair by its roots, and I'm sure it would accept the offering like rainwater.

CONCHITA. Well, I'm cutting my hair short like Clara Bow and that will be the end of the ritual.

JUAN JULIAN. I would offer to find a strong-looking tree. But the ritual won't count if it's not done on February second.

CONCHITA. I believe everything counts if you have faith.

JUAN JULIAN. So are you telling me that I should pick a strong-looking tree?

CONCHITA. Yes, if you wish.

JUAN JULIAN. And why me?

CONCHITA. Because you offer to. And you are the reader of the love stories, and anybody who dedicates his life to reading books believes in rescuing things from oblivion.

JUAN JULIAN. So is there a story in your hair?

CONCHITA. There will be the day I cut it, and that story will come to an end.

JUAN JULIAN. And how does one read the story of your hair?

CONCHITA. The same way one reads a face or a book.

JUAN JULIAN. Then we shouldn't bury your hair under a tree. We should place it inside a manuscript. The same way Victorian women used to press flowers or a lock of hair between the pages of a book.

CONCHITA. Then I would leave it to you to choose the book.

JUAN JULIAN. How about this one?

CONCHITA. My hair will be in good company with *Anna Karenina*.

JUAN JULIAN. Then close your eyes and choose a page. *(Conchita closes her eyes. She opens the book and chooses a page. Juan Julian reads:)* "At first Anna sincerely thought that she was annoyed because he insisted on pursuing her; but very soon after her return from Moscow, when she went to an evening party where she expected to see him, but which he did not attend, she came to the realization by the sadness that overwhelmed her, that she was deceiving herself."

CONCHITA. Then here, cut my hair. *(Conchita hands him the scissors. She loosens her hair and turns her back to him. He combs her hair with his fingers. He kisses her shoulder. She then turns around to return his kiss.)*

ACT TWO

Scene 1

Darkness. Music. As the lights start to come up, we hear the recorded voice of the lector narrating a passage from Anna Karenina.

JUAN JULIAN. *(Recorded voice.)* "Anna Karenina had stepped into a new life and she could not convey through words her sense of shame, rapture and horror, and she did not want to talk about it and profane this feeling through simple words. And as time passed by, the next day and the next, she still could not find the proper words to express the complexity of her feelings, and could not even find thoughts with which to reflect on all that was in her soul." *(Juan Julian and Conchita are at the factory making love. She is lying on top of a table, half naked, her skirt tucked up. He is there between her legs, shirtless and full of sweat. They have transgressed the limits of their bodies, and he now kisses her gently.)* I'd like to stop seeing you here.
CONCHITA. And where do you want to meet?
JUAN JULIAN. In my room where we could be —
CONCHITA. That would be impossible. *(They start dressing.)*
JUAN JULIAN. Then we should meet in a hotel.
CONCHITA. Hotels are cold and impersonal like hospitals.
JUAN JULIAN. Like hospitals?
CONCHITA. Yes. Every guest is looking for a remedy, whether it's a temporary relief from the world or a temporary rest from life.
JUAN JULIAN. *(Touching her face playfully.)* Then we should meet in a hospital, because sometimes I detect sad trees in your eyes after we make love.
CONCHITA. Then I must have a terrible malady.
JUAN JULIAN. Yes, and I recommend that you buy a canary and hear it sing five minutes a day ... *(He starts kissing her neck.)*
CONCHITA. And what if I can't find a canary?
JUAN JULIAN. Then you must come hear me sing when I take a

shower. *(We hear people outside.)*

CONCHITA. Go … Go … Someone's coming … Go … *(We hear Cheché in an argument. Juan Julian takes his shirt and rushes out. Conchita fixes her dress and her hair, then runs to sit at her table.)*

CHECHÉ. Wait … wait … You don't let me finish! You don't let me finish! That's one of the problems that we have, I own shares in this factory and now that your husband … *(The cigar workers enter and gather around Cheché. Next to him is a large machine wrapped in paper. There is a heated controversy over the machine. We hear the workers complaining.)*

OFELIA. I'm the owner of the factory and I have the last word …

CHECHÉ. But Ofelia …

OFELIA. Someone go upstairs and call Santiago!

CHECHÉ. Ofelia … All I'm trying to say is that all these other companies are succeeding …

PALOMO. But, Cheché, that has nothing to do with machines …

OFELIA. I don't want to listen to this. He's not the owner of this factory. Will someone call my husband! *(Cheché stands up on a chair and addresses the crowd:)*

CHECHÉ. Just let me talk!!! Let's back up here! I'm trying to make a point, and you don't let me speak …

MARELA. Let the man talk, Mamá!

CHECHÉ. Ofelia … Ofelia … All these other cigar companies have the leads. I can name them all: Caprichos, Entreactos, Petit Bouquet, Regalia de Salón, Coquetas, Conchas Finas … They all have the leads …

OFELIA. Bah! They don't roll cigars like we do.

CHECHÉ. It doesn't matter how they roll their cigars. That's what I'm trying to tell you.

OFELIA. It matters to us.

CHECHÉ. Then we're never going to get anywhere.

OFELIA. And who's in a hurry to get anywhere? Are you going somewhere, Conchita?

CONCHITA. No.

OFELIA. Are you going somewhere, Palomo?

PALOMO. I wouldn't mind going to the Canary Islands to see my grandma … *(Laughter from the crowd.)*

OFELIA. In that case I want to go to Spain …

MARELA. And I'd like to go to Russia … *(Laughter from the crowd. Juan Julian enters.)*

CHECHÉ. I'm not joking. I'm talking about the modern world.

Modernity. Progress. Advancement.

OFELIA. If working with machines means being modern then we're not interested in the modern world. *(Applause from the workers.)*

CONCHITA. Bravo!

CHECHÉ. Do you want to see our sales records? Do you want to see our records?

OFELIA. I don't have to see the sales records. I know how much we sell and we're not doing that badly.

CHECHÉ. How can we be doing well when we had to let go of two employees?

MARELA. One employee, Cheché. The other one was your wife and she left of her own accord. *(Laughter from the workers.)*

CHECHÉ. My point is that machines …

PALOMO. Machines are stealing our jobs.

MARELA. That's right. *(The crowd is getting anxious.)*

CHECHÉ. I've been given more shares in this factory. I'm — *(He is interrupted.)* Wait a second. And from now on I'm going to set things straight. *(Another interruption.)* Hold on! Do you want to know the problems we have with our factory? Do you want to know? We are stuck in time. And why are we stuck in time? We are operating in the same manner that we were twenty, thirty, fifty years ago … *(Another interruption.)* Hold on … Hold on … And why are we stuck? We are stuck because we are not part of the new century. Because we are still rolling cigars the same way that Indians rolled them hundreds of years ago. I mean, we might as well wear feathers and walk half naked with bones in our noses. There are machines that do tobacco stuffing at the speed of light: bunching machines, stripping machines …

OFELIA. And with all those machines, do they have any workers left?

CHECHÉ. Are you kidding me! The workers operate the machines. The workers run the machines.

PALOMO. Leonardo over at the Aurora factory says …

CHECHÉ. Ah, Leonardo is a lector! What does he know about machines?

PALOMO. He doesn't talk about machines like you do. But I can tell you what he says. He's always talking about maintaining our ways. Our methods. The old process we use. What we brought with us from the island. *(Raises his hands.)* We brought these to roll our cigars, so we don't need an apparatus or whatever you want to call it … *(Assertive comments from the crowd.)*

CHECHÉ. Leonardo is a lector. That's why he doesn't value machines. The lectors are being fired from all the factories, because nobody can hear them read over the sound of the machines. And that's another thing I wanted to talk about. I don't know about the rest of you, but I'm not interested in giving any more money from my pocket, from my wages to listen to a lector read me romantic novels.

CONCHITA. It's literature, Cheché. *(Palomo looks at his wife, then turns to look at Juan Julian.)*

CHECHÉ. Literature, romance novels ... It's all the same to me ...

MARELA. No. It's not the same. We learn things. And the words he reads are like a breeze that breaks the monotony of this factory.

CHECHÉ. Well, some of these companies have done away ...

JUAN JULIAN. Señor Chester, allow me to say something. My father used to say that the tradition of having readers in the factories goes back to the Taino Indians. He used to say that tobacco leaves whisper the language of the sky. And that's because through the language of cigar smoke the Indians used to communicate to the gods. Obviously I'm not an Indian, but as a lector I am a distant relative of the Cacique, the Chief Indian, who used to translate the sacred words of the deities. The workers are the *oidores*. The ones who listen quietly, the same way Taino Indians used to listen. And this is the tradition that you're trying to destroy with your machine. Instead of promoting and popularizing machines, why don't you advertise our cigars? Or are you working for the machine industry?

OFELIA. He's right. We need more advertising, so we can sell more cigars.

JUAN JULIAN. Let's face it, Chester, workers, cigars aren't popular anymore. Moving pictures now feature their stars smoking cigarettes: Valentino, Douglas Fairbanks ... They are all smoking little fags and not cigars. You can go to Hollywood and offer our cigars to producers.

CHECHÉ. You're being cynical ...

JUAN JULIAN. No, I'm warning you. This fast mode of living with machines and moving cars affects cigar consumption. And do you want to know why, Señor Chester? Because people prefer a quick smoke, the kind you get from a cigarette. The truth is that machines, cars, are keeping us from taking walks and sitting on park benches, smoking a cigar slowly and calmly. The way they should be smoked. So you see, Chester, you want modernity, and modernity is actually destroying our very own industry. The very act of smoking a cigar. *(All the workers applaud except for Cheché and Palomo.)*

OFELIA. Bravo!

JUAN JULIAN. I can certainly step out of the room if you want to take a vote. *(Juan Julian puts his hat on and starts to exit.)*

OFELIA. You don't have to go out of the room. It's obvious that we want you to stay.

JUAN JULIAN. No, let's do it the democratic way. We are in America. I'll step out of the room and you vote. Go ahead, Chester. *(Santiago enters.)*

SANTIAGO. What's going on here?

OFELIA. Ah, good! I'm glad you're here. We are about to take a vote.

SANTIAGO. What are you voting for?

OFELIA. Machines. Cheché brought a stuffing machine.

SANTIAGO. And do the workers want machines?

WORKERS. *(In unison.)* No.

SANTIAGO. So what are you voting for?

OFELIA. To do it the American way.

SANTIAGO. And what's the American way if everybody said no?

OFELIA. You talk to Cheché. Everything has gone up to his head. He also wants to get rid of the lector.

CHECHÉ. Wait a minute …

SANTIAGO. Is that true, Cheché?

CHECHÉ. I asked the workers if they wanted to continue to pay for the lector. That's all I did.

JUAN JULIAN. And I was about to go out, so the workers could vote.

SANTIAGO. You don't have to go anywhere. You stay here. I am glad to meet you. I am Santiago.

JUAN JULIAN. Juan Julian Rios, at your service.

SANTIAGO. *(To the workers.)* I've heard that many factories are getting rid of their lectors. But is this what we want, workers? Let's raise our hands if this is what we want. *(Cheché and Palomo are the only ones who raise their hands. Conchita is shocked to see Palomo's decision.)* Two votes. Then that's the answer. We are not getting rid of Juan Julian. And I have good news, workers. We are coming up with a new cigar brand and it will be called Anna Karenina.

OFELIA. Bravo!

SANTIAGO. And Marela, if you will do us the honor, I would like you to pose as Anna Karenina for the label.

MARELA. Me?

SANTIAGO. If you like.

MARELA. Of course!

SANTIAGO. Here are some clothes for you to wear. *(Santiago gives her a box. She opens the box, which contains an elegant winter coat with fur trimming and a fancy fur hat.)*

MARELA. I'll go try them on. *(She exits. Santiago addresses the workers:)*

SANTIAGO. Tomorrow we will start making plans for production. We have much work ahead of us, workers. But I promise that we will all benefit from the fruit of our work. I'm glad to be back. *(Applause from the workers. They exit. Cheché pulls Santiago aside. Santiago hands him an envelope.)* What are you voting for?

CHECHÉ. Santiago, what is this new cigar brand that you're talking about? We don't have the money …

SANTIAGO. And what is this apparatus that you've brought to our factory?

CHECHÉ. Santiago, the sales are down. You haven't been here … The price of tobacco coming from Cuba is sky high …

SANTIAGO. Should we spend our money buying machines then?

CHECHÉ. We can benefit …

SANTIAGO. It's out of the question. Return that apparatus to the factory where you got it from. And get me a calendar.

CHECHÉ. But Santiago …

SANTIAGO. Here's your money. I got a loan, Cheché. This time I'm betting my money on the factory. Get me a calendar, I said. *(Cheché runs to get a calendar. He hands it to Santiago.)* What's today's date?

CHECHÉ. The twenty-first.

SANTIAGO. How can it be the twenty-first when you've already crossed out the twenty-first on the calendar?

CHECHÉ. That's how I do it.

SANTIAGO. You've already crossed out today's date!

CHECHÉ. I know.

SANTIAGO. You might have a problem, Cheché.

CHECHÉ. And what kind of problem do you think I might have?

SANTIAGO. You are crossing out the new day before you start taking part in it.

CHECHÉ. What's the use anyway when nothing changes in this place?

SANTIAGO. That's not a good attitude.

CHECHÉ. Then what do you want me to do?

SANTIAGO. For one thing, get rid of this crap. Why don't you get the kind of calendar I have? The kind that you tear off the pages.

CHECHÉ. And do you think the page of a calendar can make a difference in one's life?

SANTIAGO. Of course. Something as simple as crossing out your days before you live them can have an effect on the mind. It can cause apprehension, anxiety and even despair.

CHECHÉ. Then I'm going straight to hell, 'cause everything here feels the same. Today feels like yesterday and the day before that.

SANTIAGO. What in the world is wrong with you, Cheché?

CHECHÉ. This factory. I can't stand it. Working here is like hitting my head against a wall … I try to make changes, modernize this place. But it's like facing a wall of concrete every time I try to do something.

SANTIAGO. Is that what it is, Chester?

CHECHÉ. Well, then there's Mildred. Ever since she left me I'm not the same. Something is missing. Have you ever seen the tail of a lizard when it's been cut off? The tail twists and moves from side to side like a worm that's been removed from the soil. The thing moves on its own, like a nerve that still has life and it's looking for the rest of the body that's been slashed away. That's how I feel sometimes. I turn from side to side on my bed at night.

I wake up in the morning looking for her in the kitchen, thinking that she's there making coffee. I look for her in the garden. And then when I come here there's this moron reading the same story every day to remind me of her.

And I hate it! I hate him! It's like there's no end to it and I just want to … *(Marela enters wearing the elegant coat and fur hat. She does a turn, feeling the smooth material of the coat, enjoying the warmth it provides.)*

MARELA. How do I look, Papá?

SANTIAGO. You'll make a great Anna. But you have to wear a flower in your hair and make her look like one of our women. I'll get you a flower, my dear.

We'll talk later, Chester. We need to talk. *(Santiago exits. Cheché turns to Marela. He contemplates her beauty. Marela looks at her clothes and then she does a turn, as if she were dancing a waltz.)*

MARELA. Well, do you think I can pose for the label?

CHECHÉ. You look beautiful. *(Juan Julian enters.)*

JUAN JULIAN. Ah, who is this Russian lady?

MARELA. Do I pass the test?

JUAN JULIAN. You look wonderful. Your father is right in choosing you. It's going to be a great picture.

44

I'm looking for my book. I think I left it here.

MARELA. I didn't see it.

JUAN JULIAN. *(Looking around.)* No. It's not here. I must've left it outside. *(He exits. Marela takes off the coat and hat. Then she takes out a box and starts pasting magazine cutouts on her work table.)*

CHECHÉ. Are you staying until late tonight?

MARELA. I am.

CHECHÉ. I'm going over the books. And you?

MARELA. I'm decorating my table with pictures I like. Photographs of movie stars, and this of a street in Moscow, so I can picture the people in the novel walking through it.

CHECHÉ. You're really obsessed with this book.

MARELA. I am.

CHECHÉ. Just the book or the lector?

MARELA. That's none of your business.

CHECHÉ. But it is. I've been watching you while you work.

MARELA. And what are you doing looking at me when I work?

CHECHÉ. You have to pay less attention to the reader and more attention to what you're doing.

MARELA. Oh, you're just trying to find any excuse to get rid of the lector. Next thing, you'll tell my father that he's distracting all the workers.

CHECHÉ. As a matter of fact he is. He is distracting you. Some of the cigars you rolled today were faulty, and you're going to get the same dickens that everyone gets.

MARELA. Yes. The new lector is getting to you with *Anna Karenina*.

CHECHÉ. I don't let any book or lector get to me.

MARELA. Sure. You probably remember your wife every time he reads a page.

CHECHÉ. My wife's dead to me.

MARELA. Dead behind your eyes, so everywhere you look you see her.

CHECHÉ. Do you want to see all the cigars you've ruined?

MARELA. Show me. I pride myself in my work. I'm one of the fastest rollers in this whole place. *(Cheché pulls out a bag of cigars.)*

CHECHÉ. But fast isn't always good, Marela.

MARELA. Nothing's wrong with it.

CHECHÉ. Here. Feel it. Hollow. A soft spot.

MARELA. Thank you, Chester. Is there anything else? Can I start pasting…?

45

CHECHÉ. As a matter of fact there's something else ...

MARELA. What, Chester?

CHECHÉ. Sometimes you get so distracted by the Russian story that I've seen you take shortcuts when you're rolling.

MARELA. What kind of shortcuts?

CHECHÉ. Sometimes you bring a cigar to your mouth and you bite the end of it, instead of reaching for the knife.

MARELA. You've seen me do that?

CHECHÉ. Yes, I've seen you do that and a lot more.

MARELA. Really?

CHECHÉ. Yes. When your mind wanders away from your work and you go far to your own little Russia. You forget the paste jar and you lick the last tobacco leaf, as if you were sealing a letter to a lover or playing with the mustache of a Russian man. Is that what it is, little Marela, you're playing with some man in your mind and you forget that you're bringing a cigar to your mouth and licking it, instead of pasting it?

MARELA. *(Laughs.)* Oh, Chester ...

CHECHÉ. Do you actually forget that you are working in a little factory where it gets real hot in the summer, and we have to wet the tobacco leaves, because they get dry from the heat and they need moisture, like the wet lick of your tongue.

MARELA. Don't look at me that way, Chester.

CHECHÉ. *(Touching her hair.)* And how do you want me to look at you?

MARELA. Don't touch me. *(She moves away. He follows her.)*

CHECHÉ. Why not?

MARELA. Because I don't like it.

CHECHÉ. But I do. Every time I listen to that story I do see my wife ... *(He moves closer to her.)*

MARELA. Get away from me! *(He tries to kiss her. She struggles to get away from him.)*

CHECHÉ. Marela, please. Come close ... You don't know ...

MARELA. Get away from me! Get away from me! *(She pushes him away. He falls to the floor.)* Don't you ever touch me again! *(Marela exits. Cheché remains on the floor. Music plays. Lights change.)*

Scene 2

Spotlight on Juan Julian sitting on a chair. He begins to recite a passage from Anna Karenina. *He remains isolated from the action of the scene.*

JUAN JULIAN. "Anna Karenina's husband did not see anything peculiar or improper in his wife's sitting together with Vronsky at a separate table and having a lively conversation with him; but he noticed that the others sitting in the drawing room considered it peculiar and improper, and so it seemed improper to him, too. He decided that he must have a conversation with his wife about it." *(Conchita enters. She goes to her table and begins to roll cigars. Palomo enters. He is like a lost animal. Juan Julian continues to read in silence.)*
PALOMO. At what time do you meet your lover?
CONCHITA. At the agreed time.
PALOMO. And what time is that?
CONCHITA. It changes like the moon.
PALOMO. Where do you meet besides this place?
CONCHITA. I can't tell you these things.
PALOMO. Why not?
CONCHITA. Because that's the way it is.
PALOMO. Does he read to you?
CONCHITA. Sometimes when he says that I look sad.
PALOMO. You get sad.
CONCHITA. It's not sadness. Sometimes I feel frightened.
PALOMO. Frightened of what?
CONCHITA. Frightened of something I have never felt or done before.
PALOMO. But isn't this what you wanted?
CONCHITA. Yes. But sometimes I can't help the guilt.
PALOMO. And how does he respond when you tell him this?
CONCHITA. He tells me that we have to make love all over again. That I have to get used to it. To him. To his body.
PALOMO. And what else does he say to you?
CONCHITA. He says things a woman likes to hear.
PALOMO. Like what?

CONCHITA. That I taste sweet and mysterious like the water hidden inside fruits and that our love will be white and pure like tobacco flowers. And it will grow at night, the same way that tobacco plants grow at night.

PALOMO. And what else does he tell you?

CONCHITA. Private things.

PALOMO. Like what?

CONCHITA. Obscenities.

PALOMO. And you like that?

CONCHITA. He knows when and how to say them.

PALOMO. And when does he talk to you this way?

CONCHITA. When we're both deep inside each other and we could almost surrender to death. When he pounds so hard inside me as if to kill me. As if to revive me from that drowning place, from that deep place where he takes me.

PALOMO. I see.

CONCHITA. Why so curious, Palomo?

PALOMO. Because I don't know … Because … You seem different. You've changed.

CONCHITA. It happens when lovers do what they are supposed to do.

PALOMO. Do you ever talk to him about me?

CONCHITA. Yes. He wanted to know why you stopped loving me.

PALOMO. And what did you tell him?

CONCHITA. I told him that it just happened one day, like everything else in life.

PALOMO. And what was his response?

CONCHITA. He wanted to know what I felt and I told him the truth. I told him that I desire and love you just the same.

PALOMO. And was he fine with that?

CONCHITA. He told me to show him how I love you. To show him on his body.

PALOMO. And what did you do?

CONCHITA. It was terrifying.

PALOMO. What was terrifying?

CONCHITA. I thought it would be impossible. That nobody could occupy that space in me. But he did. He did. And everything seemed so recognizable, as if he had known me all along. His room became a theatre and his bed a stage, and we became like actors in a play. Then I asked him to play my role, to pretend to be me and I dressed him in my clothes. And he was compliant. It was as if I was making love to myself, because he knew what to do, where to go and where to take me.

PALOMO. Show me.

CONCHITA. Show you what?

PALOMO. Show me ... Show me what he did to you and how he did it.

CONCHITA. You would have to do as actors do.

PALOMO. And what is that?

CONCHITA. Actors surrender. They stop playing themselves and they give in. You would have to let go of yourself and enter the life of another human being, and in this case it would be me.

PALOMO. Teach me then.

CONCHITA. Here, in the factory?

PALOMO. Yes, back there, where you meet him. *(Soft music plays. Conchita traces Palomo's neck and shoulders with her hand. He leads her out of the room. Lights change. Juan Julian closes the book. The soft music fades.)*

Scene 3

A danzón *plays. It's the inauguration of the new cigar brand. There's a party. The workers start filing in, dressed in their best clothes. Santiago and Ofelia enter with two bottles of rum and glasses.*

OFELIA. Did you get enough rum, Santiago?

SANTIAGO. Did I get enough rum? Tell her how much rum I got, Juan Julian.

JUAN JULIAN. He's got enough rum to get an elephant drunk.

OFELIA. Then give me some before anybody gets here, so I can calm my nerves.

SANTIAGO. What are you nervous about?

OFELIA. Oh, I have the heart of a seal and when I get excited it wants to swim out of my chest. *(Santiago gives her a drink.)*

SANTIAGO. Let's have a drink, the three of us. We ought to have a private toast before anybody gets here. *(Santiago serves drinks.)* We really haven't done that badly this year. Sales were down last month but we're still staying above water.

OFELIA. We'll do well, Santiago. People need to blow out smoke and vent themselves.

SANTIAGO. *(Toasting.)* That's right, salud!

OFELIA. Salud.

JUAN JULIAN. Salud.

OFELIA. Let's bring out the lanterns. *(The three of them exit. Cheché and Palomo, both elegantly dressed, enter with palm leaves to decorate the factory. They are engaged in conversation.)*

PALOMO. Sometimes I don't know what to do ... I can feel it. Or it's just me. My mind. At night I can't sleep. I lie there awake thinking, imagining the two of them together. I can still smell him on her skin, her clothes and her handkerchief. I can see him on her face and her eyes, and I don't know what to do ...

CHECHÉ. You should move up North to Trenton and start a new life. Take her away from here. That's what I wanted to do with Mildred. I'd figure we could live up North. The two of us could work in a cigar factory. There are plenty of them in Trenton. And there are no lectors and no good-for-nothing love stories, which put ideas into women's heads and ants inside their pants ... *(Juan Julian enters with a garland of Chinese lanterns.)*

JUAN JULIAN. Would you give me a hand with the lanterns?

PALOMO. Ah, we were just talking about the love stories.

JUAN JULIAN. It's obvious that you don't care much for them. You almost made me lose my job the other day.

PALOMO. Oh, I'm curious as to how the story ends.

CHECHÉ. Yeah! Does the husband ever think of killing the lover? *(Laughs.)* I would've killed the bastard a long time ago.

JUAN JULIAN. The husband would probably choose a duel, instead of killing the lover in cold blood.

CHECHÉ. I would've shot the son of a bitch a long time ago.

JUAN JULIAN. But that's not the way things were done in those days.

CHECHÉ. Then the husband is a coward and a stinker.

PALOMO. Oh, I don't see the husband as a coward. He might be more clever than the three of us. Wouldn't you say so, Juan Julian?

JUAN JULIAN. Well, the husband is acting according to his status. He is a man of power. He has one of the most important positions in the ministry. And we're talking about Saint Petersburg society — everyone knows each other and he doesn't want Anna's affair to turn into a big scandal.

CHECHÉ. The husband is a pansy if you ask me.

PALOMO. So what character do you identify with in the novel?

JUAN JULIAN. I like them all. I learn things from all of them.

PALOMO. And what have you learned from Anna's lover?

JUAN JULIAN. Oh, I don't know … I …

PALOMO. I'm intrigued as to how he became interested in her. *(Juan Julian knows where Palomo is trying to go with this.)*

JUAN JULIAN. Well, it's very obvious in the novel.

PALOMO. And what's your personal opinion?

JUAN JULIAN. She came to him because she thought that he could help her.

PALOMO. Help her how?

JUAN JULIAN. Help her to love again. Help her to recognize herself as a woman all over again. She had probably known only one man and that was the husband. With the lover she learns a new way of loving. And it's this new way of loving that makes her go back to the lover over and over again. But that's my interpretation. *(Santiago and Ofelia enter.)*

SANTIAGO. Good! You are all here. We are celebrating the whole day today. Let's have another drink.

OFELIA. Remember you have a speech to make.

SANTIAGO. *(Lifting the bottle.)* This will inspire me.

OFELIA. At the rate we're going we'll be drunk before the party gets started.

SANTIAGO. *(Laughs.)* Enjoy yourself. Today I'm the happiest man on earth. *(Conchita enters. She's dressed in a chiffon paisley dress.)*

CONCHITA. Are you drinking without me?

SANTIAGO. Of course not. Come have a drink with us. Where's your sister? You look beautiful in that dress, my child. I've never seen you wear it.

CONCHITA. Papá, just a month ago I wore it. We were invited to a party. I remember as if it were yesterday. *(She looks at her mother.)* Mamá hates paisleys.

OFELIA. No, I don't, my child.

CONCHITA. You said I looked like an old lady the last time I wore it.

OFELIA. Frankly, I just didn't think much of it when you had it made. But now that you cut your hair and you look so different, it's actually very becoming.

PALOMO. You do look beautiful, my love.

OFELIA. I like paisleys.

51

CONCHITA. They remind me of gypsies and bohemians.

PALOMO. You actually look very bohemian.

JUAN JULIAN. It's true. Paisleys look dreamy, as if they come from a floating world. *(Palomo looks at Juan Julian. Juan Julian lifts his glass. Palomo brings Conchita close to him and wraps his arm around her.)* Señores, one question. As an outsider, as a foreigner in this country, I have something to ask. Why do Americans prohibit something as divine as whiskey and rum?

SANTIAGO. Because Americans become socialists when they drink. *(Laughter from the crowd.)*

PALOMO. I have another answer to your question. Alcohol is prohibited in this country because alcohol is like literature. Literature brings out the best and the worst part of ourselves. If you're angry it brings out your anger. If you are sad, it brings out your sadness. And some of us are … Let's just say, not very happy. *(Ofelia, who is a little tipsy, taps her glass to make a speech.)*

OFELIA. *(Doing a dance step.)* Ah, but rum brings out your best steps if you are a good dancer. If you have two left feet, it's better if you don't dance at all. So let's face it, señores, Americans are good at making movies, radios and cars, but when it comes to dancing, it's better if … With the exception of the colored folks, of course. They've got what it takes to dance up a storm. That's why I think alcohol is prohibited, because most Americans don't know how to dance. *(Grabbing Santiago by the hand.)* Let's go, I feel like dancing.

SANTIAGO. No. We can't dance yet, because I have an announcement to make. Where's Marela?

OFELIA. She must be putting on her costume.

SANTIAGO. Well, señoras y señores, today we've taken time from work to drink and dance, and to celebrate the new cigar brand we are launching into the market. *(He takes out a cigar from his shirt pocket.)* This well-crafted cigar is wrapped in the finest leaves from Vuelta Abajo in Pinar del Río, the tip of the island of Cuba. The length of this new cigar is six and one-eighth inches. The ring gauge is fifty-two. I truly believe this is our finest *toro*.

Where's Marela? She should be here. *(Marela enters dressed in an elegant black gown. She is like Anna on the night of the ball.)*

MARELA. I'm here, Papá.

SANTIAGO. Let me look at you, my little blue sky.

OFELIA. But my child, you look beautiful.

SANTIAGO. You came just in time … I was just about to say that since most cigars are named after women and romantic love stories, today we are baptizing our new cigar with the name Anna Karenina! This cigar will sell for ten cents and we are hoping this new brand will bring us fortune and prosperity. So now that we are all gathered here, I would like to ask my beloved Ofelia to do us the honor of officially lighting the first Anna Karenina. *(Applause from the crowd. The cigar is passed to Ofelia. Santiago lights it with a match. Ofelia takes a puff and blows out a ring of smoke.)* Well?

OFELIA. It's … It's … Aaaah! It burns like a blue dream. *(The crowd applauds.)*

PALOMO. Bravo! Bravo! *(Ofelia passes the cigar to Santiago and he gives it to Marela.)*

SANTIAGO. And to the youngest one in the family, our very own Anna. *(Marela takes a puff, coughs a little. She laughs.)*

MARELA. Mhm! Lovely! *(She passes the cigar to another. This person presents it to Santiago. Santiago takes a puff.)*

SANTIAGO. Ah! It's glorious. Perfecto. *(Applause from the crowd.)* Chester. *(Santiago hands the cigar to someone, who passes it to Cheché. He takes a puff.)*

CHECHÉ. Burns well. Pleasant aroma. I detect a little bit of cherry. I think it's our finest horse. *(Applause. The cigar is passed to Palomo. Palomo passes it to Conchita. She takes a puff.)*

CONCHITA. Ah! It speaks of forests and orchids. *(Applause. Conchita hands the cigar to Marela. Marela gives it to Palomo. He takes a puff.)*

PALOMO. Mhm! Magnifico! Definitely like aged rum. Sweet like mangoes. *(Palomo passes it to Santiago.)*

SANTIAGO. You forgot Juan Julian.

PALOMO. Ah, yes we can't forget our lector, who brought us the world of *Anna Karenina*. *(Santiago passes the cigar back to Palomo. Palomo takes off his hat and gives Juan Julian the cigar. This is an offense since the cigar should never be handed directly to the person that is supposed to smoke. There has to be a mediator to facilitate communication with the gods. Juan Julian smiles. He smells the cigar, looks up and makes a gesture to the gods.)*

JUAN JULIAN. Sweet aroma. *(Taking a puff.)* It sighs like a sunset and it has a little bit of cocoa beans and cedar. I believe we have a cigar, señores!

SANTIAGO. We do have a cigar, señores! We have a champion!

OFELIA. *(A little tipsy.)* Indeed we have a champion!

MARELA. Papá, let's go out into the streets and tell the world about our cigar. Let's give our new cigars to the people.

SANTIAGO. And go bankrupt, my child! No, I propose a gunshot!

OFELIA. A gunshot! Santiago, you're drunk. Stop drinking.

SANTIAGO. No inauguration is complete without the breaking of a bottle or a gunshot.

MARELA. I propose two gunshots then!

SANTIAGO. Can't have two gunshots. It's got to be three.

MARELA. Then I'll shoot the third one. *(Laughter.)*

SANTIAGO. Let's go. Let's shoot!

OFELIA. Just make sure you aim up high, but don't shoot the moon! *(They all laugh. The workers bring the party outside. As Conchita starts to leave, Palomo grabs her by the arm.)*

PALOMO. Where are you going?

CONCHITA. Outside.

PALOMO. You've been looking at him the whole night. You're still in love with this man.

CONCHITA. Maybe just as much as you are.

PALOMO. I don't like men. *(Sound of a celebratory gunshot. Laughter.)*

CONCHITA. Then why do you always want me to tell you what I do with him?

PALOMO. Because it's part of the old habit we have of listening. We are listeners.

CONCHITA. No, there's something else.

PALOMO. You're right there's something else. And it's terrible sometimes.

CONCHITA. Then nothing makes sense to me anymore. *(Another gunshot. More laughter.)*

PALOMO. *(Grabbing her arm.)* I want you to go back to him and tell him you want to make love like a knife.

CONCHITA. Why a knife?

PALOMO. Because everything has to be killed. *(Another gunshot. More laughter. Ofelia, Santiago, Marela and Juan Julian reenter.)*

OFELIA. Señores, I have a confession to make. When I was seventeen, and that was yesterday, I was chosen to pose for a cigar brand that was called Aida, like the opera. And, of course, just the thought of my face being on a cigar ring and in so many men's hands and lips, my mother was scandalized. You see, we weren't cigar people, we were in the guava jelly business. So when my mother forbid me to pose for the label, I told her that I wanted a picture of my face on a can of guava marmalade. And it was only fair. So, they dressed me up in a red dress and I had a red carnation behind my ear. They had me looking lovely sitting in a hammock and a parrot by my side … *(Everyone laughs.)*

SANTIAGO. Let's go, my dear. We have smoked, we have fired a gun and you've had too much to drink.

OFELIA. Bah, you just want to take advantage of me because I'm drunk.

MARELA. *(Embarrassed.)* Mamá! *(Santiago laughs. He takes Ofelia by the hand. They start to exit.)*

SANTIAGO. Good night!

MARELA. Good night!

OFELIA. Marela, are you coming with us?

MARELA. I'll be there in a minute.

OFELIA. Don't be too long. *(They exit.)*

PALOMO. *(Grabbing Conchita's hand.)* Let's go home. *(To the others.)* We'll see you tomorrow.

JUAN JULIAN. Adios!

CONCHITA. Adios! *(Conchita and Palomo exit, leaving Marela and Juan Julian alone.)*

MARELA. Oh, I don't want this night to end. I could stay up all night. I don't want to sleep. We sleep too much. We spend more than a third of our lives sleeping, sleeping. Darkness descends and everything is a mystery to us. We don't know if trees really walk at night, as I've heard in legends. We don't really know if statues and spirits dance in the squares unbeknown to us. And how would we ever know if we sleep? We sleep and sleep …

JUAN JULIAN. Oh, I want to have what you drank. What did you drink?

MARELA. Oh, I didn't drink. I just feel gladness.

Papá was so happy. I like to see him that way. And Mamá was so full of joy. *(Laughs.)* She's the one who drinks a little too much.

JUAN JULIAN. It's good to drink a little once in a while. *(Cheché reenters. He stays at a distance, watching.)*

MARELA. Yes, we deserve a little drink. We work hard enough. We deserve all that life offers us, and life is made of little moments. Little moments as small as violet petals. Little moments I could save in a jar and keep forever, like now talking to you.

JUAN JULIAN. *(Playfully.)* Ah! So you are a collector. And what sort of things do you like to collect besides a night like this one?

MARELA. The first time you read and the day you walked me to the pharmacy.

JUAN JULIAN. So I'm in one of your jars.

MARELA. In many.

JUAN JULIAN. *(Smiles.)* Many. *(Beat. Looks at her tenderly.)* You are clear and fresh as water. Did anybody ever tell you this?

MARELA. No, never.

JUAN JULIAN. Then people are blind.

MARELA. Blind? Do you think so? And how can one teach the blind to see?

JUAN JULIAN. I wouldn't know. I'm not blind.

MARELA. But we are all blind in the eyes of those who can't see.

JUAN JULIAN. You're right.

MARELA. We just have to learn to use our eyes in the dark. We have to learn to see through words and sound, through our hands. *(Touches his hand.)*

JUAN JULIAN. I'm sure those who are blind will see your beauty once they touch your face. *(Touches her face tenderly.)*

I must go now. Sleep well.

MARELA. Adios.

JUAN JULIAN. Adios. *(Just as Juan Julian is about to exit.)*

MARELA. Juan Julian ...

JUAN JULIAN. Yes.

MARELA. Lend me the book.

JUAN JULIAN. *(Not realizing that he is holding it.)* What book?

MARELA. The book in your hand.

JUAN JULIAN. Oh!

MARELA. I promise not to get ahead of the story.

JUAN JULIAN. Bring it tomorrow morning or I won't have a book to read.

MARELA. May you dream of angels!

JUAN JULIAN. *(Kissing her face.)* You, too. *(As Juan Julian exits, Marela stays looking at him in the distance. She brings the book to her chest, then she opens it and reads, as if to find consolation, the sort one seeks in the lonely hours of the night.)*

MARELA. "Anna Karenina prepared herself for the journey with joy and willfulness. With small, skillful hands she opened a red bag and took out a little cushion, which she placed on her knees before closing the bag." *(Cheché emerges from the shadows. He takes a handkerchief from his pocket and dries his face. He looks at Marela. His glance is full of desire. Marela sees him. She closes the book. Cheché grabs her arm. Blackout.)*

Scene 4

Palomo enters the factory carrying a couple of heavy boxes. Conchita is clearing up the mess from the night before.

PALOMO. Where's Cheché?

CONCHITA. He hasn't come in yet.

PALOMO. I hope someone gets here with the keys to the safe. The boy who delivered these boxes is out there and he wants to get paid.

CONCHITA. I'll go to the house and ask Mamá for the keys.

PALOMO. No. You got to help me take inventory of all these boxes. *(Hands her some papers.)*

CONCHITA. As soon as I finish with this.

I wonder why Papá isn't here.

PALOMO. He's probably still in bed. He did drink ...

CONCHITA. Yes you're right. Mamá must be putting cold compresses on his forehead. It always happens. *(Santiago and Ofelia enter. Santiago is trying to get rid of his hangover by rubbing his forehead.)*

OFELIA. Morning!

CONCHITA. Morning!

PALOMO. Santiago, I need the key to the safe. I have to pay for this delivery.

SANTIAGO. Ofelia has them.

OFELIA. I just left them at the office on top of the desk. *(Palomo exits. Ofelia sits down and starts rolling cigars.)*

SANTIAGO. Where's Cheché?

CONCHITA. He hasn't arrived yet.

SANTIAGO. I don't blame him. I would've stayed in bed myself. But your mother is like a rooster. When she gets up from bed nobody ...

OFELIA. I didn't wake you up.

SANTIAGO. I didn't say you did. It's those slippers you use to walk around the house. They are louder than a running train. *(Makes noise.)* Shoo ... Shoo ... Everywhere ... One day I'm going to throw them out the window.

OFELIA. You do that and I'll give your Sunday shoes to the chimney cleaner.

SANTIAGO. See, now the pain got worse! This woman, how she likes to bother me! Ay!

CONCHITA. Do you want my bottle of spirits, Papá?

SANTIAGO. Give me anything you have, my child. Your mother doesn't take care of me. *(Conchita gives him the bottle of spirits. He sniffs. Marela enters wearing the long coat. She goes to her table and starts to roll cigars.)*

MARELA. Morning!

CONCHITA. Marela, why are you wearing that coat? Aren't you warm? …

MARELA. No. Some coats keep winter inside them. You wear them and you find pockets full of December, January and February. All those months that cover the earth with snow and make everything still. That's how I want to be, layered and still.

OFELIA. My child, are you all right?

MARELA. I'm fine, Mamá. Don't worry about me. *(Juan Julian enters.)*

JUAN JULIAN. Good morning!

ALL. Good morning!

MARELA. Here's your book. *(Hands him the book. Juan Julian notices Marela's coat, and that she seems to be in a state of dismay.)*

JUAN JULIAN. Thank you. *(Palomo reenters.)*

PALOMO. Has Cheché come in yet?

CONCHITA. No. He's just late. Sit down. Juan Julian is going to read to us.

JUAN JULIAN. Today I'll begin by reading Part Three, Chapter Thirteen, of *Anna Karenina*: "In his youth Anna Karenina's husband had been intrigued by the idea of dueling because he was physically a coward and was well aware of this fact. In his youth this terror had often forced him to think about dueling and imagining himself in a situation in which it was necessary to endanger his life." *(Cheché enters unnoticed. His head is heavy with dark thoughts.)* "This old ingrained feeling now reasserted itself. Let's suppose I challenge him. Let's suppose someone teaches me how to do it, he went on thinking." *(Cheché pulls out a gun.)* "They put us in position, I squeeze the trigger, he said to himself, and it turns out I've killed him. He shook his head to drive away such silly thoughts. What would be the sense of killing a man in order to define one's own relations with a woman … " *(Cheché shoots Juan Julian. Then shoots again. The sound of the gun echoes and echoes as Juan Julian falls to the floor. The workers are shocked. Some of them look up to see where the shot came from. The shot still echoes throughout the room as Marela reaches out to touch the dying lector. The lights fade to black.)*

Scene 5

Three days have passed. The factory workers are rolling cigars and organizing the tobacco leaves by their proper size and shape. Marela is still wearing her coat.

OFELIA. What silence! I never knew that silence could have so much weight. Can someone say something? Can someone read? We are listeners! We are *oidores!* I can't get used to this silence all around us. It's as if a metal blanket has fallen on us.

PALOMO. The same silence we had when our last reader died.

OFELIA. No, this silence is louder. Much louder. Much louder.

SANTIAGO. That's because Juan Julian died before his time, and the shadows of the young are heavier and they linger over the earth like a cloud.

MARELA. I should write his name on a piece of paper and place it in a glass of water with brown sugar, so his spirit knows that he is welcomed in this factory, and he can come here and drink sweet water. And nobody better tell me that it's wrong for me to do this! You hear me, Mamá! *(For the first time tears come to her eyes.)*

SANTIAGO. Your mother hasn't said anything, my child.

MARELA. I know she hasn't. But we must look after the dead, so they can feel part of the world. So they don't forget us and we could count on them when we cross to the other side.

CONCHITA. We should continue reading, Papá!

MARELA. Yes, we should continue reading the story in his honor, so he doesn't feel that he left his job undone. He should know that we're still his faithful listeners.

CONCHITA. If I could, I would read, but I know that if I open that book I'll be weak.

MARELA. We shouldn't cry. Tears are for the weak that mourn the knife and the killer, and the trickle of blood that streams from this factory all the way to the house where he was born.

OFELIA. Could someone read? *(Pause.)*

PALOMO. I will read.

OFELIA. That's it, read, so we can get rid of this silence and this heat. And we can pause over a few lines and sigh and be glad that we are alive.

SANTIAGO. Read something cheerful.

MARELA. Stories should be finished, Papá. Let him finish the book.

CONCHITA. She's right. Stories should be finished or they suffer the same fate as those who die before their time. *(Palomo opens the book. He looks at Conchita.)*

PALOMO. *Anna Karenina.* Part Three, Chapter Fourteen: "By the time he arrived in Petersburg, Anna Karenina's husband was not only completely determined to carry out his decision, but he had composed in his head a letter he would write to his wife." *(He looks up from the book and stares at Conchita.)* "In his letter he was going to write everything he'd been meaning to tell her." *(The lights begin to fade.)*

End of Play

PROPERTY LIST

Money (SANTIAGO, CHECHÉ, ELIADES)
Handkerchiefs (MARELA, CONCHITA, OFELIA, CHECHÉ)
Letter and photograph (OFELIA)
Knife (SANTIAGO)
Books strapped with a belt (JUAN JULIAN)
Shoe (CHECHÉ)
Anna Karenina (JUAN JULIAN)
Cigar papers and tobacco (OFELIA, MARELA, CHECHÉ, PALOMO, CONCHITA)
Boxes (CHECHÉ, PALOMO)
Scissors (CONCHITA)
Machine wrapped in paper (CHECHÉ)
Box with fur-trimmed coat and fur hat (SANTIAGO)
Envelope (SANTIAGO)
Calendar (CHECHÉ)
Box with magazine cutouts (MARELA)
Paste (MARELA)
Bag of cigars (CHECHÉ)
Two bottles of rum and glasses (SANTIAGO, OFELIA)
Palm leaves (CHECHÉ, PALOMO)
Garland of Chinese lanterns (JUAN JULIAN)
Cigar (SANTIAGO)
Matches (SANTIAGO)
Papers (PALOMO)
Bottle of spirits (CONCHITA)
Gun (CHECHÉ)

SOUND EFFECTS

Crowd at cockfight
Ship approaching harbor
Girl urinating
Bell ringing
Danzón music
Gunshots
Echoing gunshot

NEW PLAYS

★ **BE AGGRESSIVE by Annie Weisman.** Vista Del Sol is paradise, sandy beaches, avocado-lined streets. But for seventeen-year-old cheerleader Laura, everything changes when her mother is killed in a car crash, and she embarks on a journey to the Spirit Institute of the South where she can learn "cheer" with Bible belt intensity. "…filled with lingual gymnastics…stylized rapid-fire dialogue…" *–Variety.* "…a new, exciting, and unique voice in the American theatre…" *–BackStage West.* [1M, 4W, extras] ISBN: 0-8222-1894-1

★ **FOUR by Christopher Shinn.** Four people struggle desperately to connect in this quiet, sophisticated, moving drama. "…smart, broken-hearted…Mr. Shinn has a precocious and forgiving sense of how power shifts in the game of sexual pursuit…He promises to be a playwright to reckon with…" *–NY Times.* "A voice emerges from an American place. It's got humor, sadness and a fresh and touching rhythm that tell of the loneliness and secrets of life…[a] poetic, haunting play." *–NY Post.* [3M, 1W] ISBN: 0-8222-1850-X

★ **WONDER OF THE WORLD by David Lindsay-Abaire.** A madcap picaresque involving Niagara Falls, a lonely tour-boat captain, a pair of bickering private detectives and a husband's dirty little secret. "Exceedingly whimsical and playfully wicked. Winning and genial. A top-drawer production." *–NY Times.* "Full frontal lunacy is on display. A most assuredly fresh and hilarious tragicomedy of marital discord run amok…absolutely hysterical…" *–Variety.* [3M, 4W (doubling)] ISBN: 0-8222-1863-1

★ **QED by Peter Parnell.** Nobel Prize-winning physicist and all-around genius Richard Feynman holds forth with captivating wit and wisdom in this fascinating biographical play that originally starred Alan Alda. "QED is a seductive mix of science, human affections, moral courage, and comic eccentricity. It reflects on, among other things, death, the absence of God, travel to an unexplored country, the pleasures of drumming, and the need to know and understand." *–NY Magazine.* "Its rhythms correspond to the way that people—even geniuses—approach and avoid highly emotional issues, and it portrays Feynman with affection and awe." *–The New Yorker.* [1M, 1W] ISBN: 0-8222-1924-7

★ **UNWRAP YOUR CANDY by Doug Wright.** Alternately chilling and hilarious, this deliciously macabre collection of four bedtime tales for adults is guaranteed to keep you awake for nights on end. "Engaging and intellectually satisfying…a treat to watch." *–NY Times.* "Fiendishly clever. Mordantly funny and chilling. Doug Wright teases, freezes and zaps us." *–Village Voice.* "Four bite-size plays that bite back." *–Variety.* [flexible casting] ISBN: 0-8222-1871-2

★ **FURTHER THAN THE FURTHEST THING by Zinnie Harris.** On a remote island in the middle of the Atlantic secrets are buried. When the outside world comes calling, the islanders find their world blown apart from the inside as well as beyond. "Harris winningly produces an intimate and poetic, as well as political, family saga." *–Independent (London).* "Harris' enthralling adventure of a play marks a departure from stale, well-furrowed theatrical terrain." *–Evening Standard (London).* [3M, 2W] ISBN: 0-8222-1874-7

★ **THE DESIGNATED MOURNER by Wallace Shawn.** The story of three people living in a country where what sort of books people like to read and how they choose to amuse themselves becomes both firmly personal and unexpectedly entangled with questions of survival. "This is a playwright who does not just tell you what it is like to be arrested at night by goons or to fall morally apart and become an aimless yet weirdly contented ghost yourself. He has the originality to make you feel it." *–Times (London).* "A fascinating play with beautiful passages of writing…" *–Variety.* [2M, 1W] ISBN: 0-8222-1848-8

DRAMATISTS PLAY SERVICE, INC.
440 Park Avenue South, New York, NY 10016 212-683-8960 Fax 212-213-1539
postmaster@dramatists.com   www.dramatists.com

NEW PLAYS

★ **SHEL'S SHORTS by Shel Silverstein.** Lauded poet, songwriter and author of children's books, the incomparable Shel Silverstein's short plays are deeply infused with the same wicked sense of humor that made him famous. "…[a] childlike honesty and twisted sense of humor." *–Boston Herald.* "…terse dialogue and an absurdity laced with a tang of dread give [*Shel's Shorts*] more than a trace of Samuel Beckett's comic existentialism." *–Boston Phoenix.* [flexible casting] ISBN: 0-8222-1897-6

★ **AN ADULT EVENING OF SHEL SILVERSTEIN by Shel Silverstein.** Welcome to the darkly comic world of Shel Silverstein, a world where nothing is as it seems and where the most innocent conversation can turn menacing in an instant. These ten imaginative plays vary widely in content, but the style is unmistakable. "…[*An Adult Evening*] shows off Silverstein's virtuosic gift for wordplay…[and] sends the audience out…with a clear appreciation of human nature as perverse and laughable." *–NY Times.* [flexible casting] ISBN: 0-8222-1873-9

★ **WHERE'S MY MONEY? by John Patrick Shanley.** A caustic and sardonic vivisection of the institution of marriage, laced with the author's inimitable razor-sharp wit. "…Shanley's gift for acid-laced one-liners and emotionally tumescent exchanges is certainly potent…" *–Variety.* "…lively, smart, occasionally scary and rich in reverse wisdom." *–NY Times.* [3M, 3W] ISBN: 0-8222-1865-8

★ **A FEW STOUT INDIVIDUALS by John Guare.** A wonderfully screwy comedy-drama that figures Ulysses S. Grant in the throes of writing his memoirs, surrounded by a cast of fantastical characters, including the Emperor and Empress of Japan, the opera star Adelina Patti and Mark Twain. "Guare's smarts, passion and creativity skyrocket to awesome heights…" *–Star Ledger.* "…precisely the kind of good new play that you might call an everyday miracle…every minute of it is fresh and newly alive…" *–Village Voice.* [10M, 3W] ISBN: 0-8222-1907-7

★ **BREATH, BOOM by Kia Corthron.** A look at fourteen years in the life of Prix, a Bronx native, from her ruthless girl-gang leadership at sixteen through her coming to maturity at thirty. "…vivid world, believable and eye-opening, a place worthy of a dramatic visit, where no one would want to live but many have to." *–NY Times.* "…rich with humor, terse vernacular strength and gritty detail…" *–Variety.* [1M, 9W] ISBN: 0-8222-1849-6

★ **THE LATE HENRY MOSS by Sam Shepard.** Two antagonistic brothers, Ray and Earl, are brought together after their father, Henry Moss, is found dead in his seedy New Mexico home in this classic Shepard tale. "…His singular gift has been for building mysteries out of the ordinary ingredients of American family life…" *–NY Times.* "…rich moments …Shepard finds gold." *–LA Times.* [7M, 1W] ISBN: 0-8222-1858-5

★ **THE CARPETBAGGER'S CHILDREN by Horton Foote.** One family's history spanning from the Civil War to WWII is recounted by three sisters in evocative, intertwining monologues. "…bittersweet music—[a] rhapsody of ambivalence…in its modest, garrulous way…theatrically daring." *–The New Yorker.* [3W] ISBN: 0-8222-1843-7

★ **THE NINA VARIATIONS by Steven Dietz.** In this funny, fierce and heartbreaking homage to *The Seagull*, Dietz puts Chekhov's star-crossed lovers in a room and doesn't let them out. "A perfect little jewel of a play…" *–Shepherdstown Chronicle.* "…a delightful revelation of a writer at play; and also an odd, haunting, moving theater piece of lingering beauty." *–Eastside Journal (Seattle).* [1M, 1W (flexible casting)] ISBN: 0-8222-1891-7

DRAMATISTS PLAY SERVICE, INC.
440 Park Avenue South, New York, NY 10016 212-683-8960 Fax 212-213-1539
postmaster@dramatists.com www.dramatists.com